hell;
purgatory;
heaven;

Autobiography of Hugh M Jackson

Apart from my own, only one other character's real name is used, and that is George.

Copyright © 2023 Hugh M Jackson

All rights reserved. No part of this publication may be reproduced or transmitted in any form or by any means, electronic or mechanical including photocopying, recording or any information storage or retrieval system, without prior permission in writing from the publishers.

The right of Hugh M Jackson to be identified as the author of this work has been asserted by him in accordance with the Copyright, Designs and Patents Act 1988.

First published in the United Kingdom in 2023 by
The Choir Press

ISBN 978-1-78963-420-4

Hell; purgatory; heaven;

Introduction to
and history of
the family unit into
which I would be born

I've forgotten how many times I've told the story about my earliest recollection of life. I think the reason I remember it so well was because, in its own way, it was a frightening experience at that time.

When told now, however, it's really a rather funny story, as my fear was very apt for the situation. What's strange about the story now though, is that it's not, after all, my earliest recollection of life.

Prior to relating that story once more, however, I think it's appropriate that you get to know more about the family unit into which I would be born, and how my life would become shaped, or manipulated, by each and every member of a family who perceived themselves as being better than any of their neighbours.

It's important to note that most of the information mentioned in the next few paragraphs was stuff which only became known to me as I was growing up, in some cases, into my teenage years.

Just three months after their marriage, a child came into the lives of my future parents.

In January 1937, they gave birth to their first child, a boy, who throughout this story will only be referred to as Bro.1.

Their next born was also a boy (referred to as Bro.2), born in 1941. It seems that, in the years between those births, there had been some miscarriages, all girls. Apparently, there was some medical reason which prevented my mother-to-be from successfully carrying a female child.

My future parents' ideal family, it seems, could only be achieved by having the gift of a daughter. With that in mind, and their previous miscarriage history, it would take a miracle for their ideal family to be achieved.

How anyone could believe the existing "room and kitchen" type of housing of those days could be regarded as an acceptable form of accommodation is beyond comprehension.

The room was accurately described. It needed the purchase of a bed and some wardrobe and drawer space. Those were essential items. If you could afford maybe a couple of chairs plus some other nick-nacks, that would be it furnished.

Additionally, the room had what was called a "set-in" bed within its boundaries. This was a built-in bed within an alcove and was separated from the rest of the room by just a curtain.

Typical usage might have been the parents sleeping behind a curtain in the set-in bed, with the grown-up married couple in the other bed. In those days married children had to continue to live with their parents for quite a few years as there was insufficient housing stock available.

I'm not sure how any intimate moments would have transpired between either couple, under those circumstances.

The only other room, the kitchen, was somewhat misdescribed in my opinion, way back in those days.

Cooking and heating were both supplied by a range-type stove which was coal-fired, and chairs would be relatively close to that source of heat, which failed to permeate through to the bedroom area.

Taking up a relative amount of space would be a table, and also a cabinet for storing food items as well as crockery, utensils, and cleaning materials.

The coal supply which served the range was also

stored in a built-in bunker within this kitchen. The coal was carried on a shovel past the table and chairs with the likelihood some of it would spill onto the carpet and furniture during its journey to the range stove.

There was a single sash window in this room which was reached by stretching over a small sink which delivered only cold water.

If hot water was required it had to be boiled in a pot, or whistling kettle, then transferred to the sink. This sink was used very often, and for a wide range of duties: for example, washing dishes, preparing vegetables, washing hair, shaving, personal body washing (as there was no bath or shower) even though this was the main room where everyone would congregate.

The toilet was not located within the house, but out on the communal landing outside of the house and was to be shared by all persons living within each of the properties on that landing.

It was effectively just the size of a small cupboard which housed only a water closet. That was probably where the phrase W.C. originated.

Toilet paper was usually torn-up newspaper on a string for the most part, as no household would pay for proper toilet paper only for it to disappear into some other neighbour's house. There was no hand-washing facility within this space, nor any bath or shower in any of the individual dwellings.

Outside, at the back of the blocks of flats, was where residents of every dwelling would take their turn in the washhouses to do their laundry. Many arguments took place as folk "stole" the allocated day or time when another resident was due their turn to do their washing and drying. Ladies also had to carry down their own clothesline on which to hang the washed items. More arguments ensued as others put their washing line on top of yours on the clothes poles, meaning you couldn't then untie your rope to return it safely back home.

There were still other inter-family disputes as kids from other flats played football through the various lines of washed laundry, thereby rendering some items to need re-washing.

With the commencement of World War 2, my father-to-be was conscripted into the army and then sent to the front line. Family life then consisted of my mother-to-be raising her two boys with the help of her own mother and her sisters, each of whom had their own kids to look after and support.

After WW2 had ended, there was the need for a lot of building works to replace any homes which had been destroyed or damaged, but also to accommodate other families whose children had grown during those war years and who now needed their own age-related privacy.

The "room and kitchen" style of housing was now obsolete and outdated, and modern standards were designed and required to be built urgently.

hell;

When the war was over, my father-to-be returned safely home, and in 1947 their family was added to when I was born. It's probably fair to say they were over the moon at that point, but not really because of my birth. Their ecstasy was most definitely because I was a twin, and on this occasion, the first-born was a girl. It seems that she had somehow been protected because she was in the womb along with me, a boy.

Because of my presence, their miracle had happened, and their ideal family had been achieved. They had their longed-for gift of a daughter, their "golden child".

Following my birth, our family then consisted of a father; a mother; Bro.1 who was ten years of age; Bro.2 who was six; my twin sister; and me, the baby of the family.

It is well documented and recognised that, in the case of twins, the second-born child would be the one most likely to have health problems.

Within such a family unit, there should surely have been a loving, caring, family future to look forward to as I grew up through childhood and into adulthood.

There were, of course, some life events which even the most loving of families could not prevent from taking place. One such event happened to me at a very young age, and this would have a profound effect on me throughout the rest of my life.

I was just one and a half years of age on New Year's Day in 1949 and was on the operating table in the local hospital having a mastoid operation. There was no threat to my life, but the operation was regarded as having been unsuccessful because I would have a frequent discharge from that ear for evermore.

The discharge could happen at any time and anywhere. The maintenance procedure was to clean the ear twice daily, and then insert cotton wool into the ear to contain any new leakage within the ear cavity.

Around the age of six or seven, my mother decided it was time for me to take ownership of this maintenance myself. I should state at this point that my mother had never given me any information in respect of the fact that I had ever undergone that operation, nor indeed, what had transpired during it.

Since the maintenance had been routinely conducted twice daily throughout the preceding years, it was something I just had to continue to do, and therefore I felt no need to ask for any explanation relating to why this had to be the case.

Going forward, throughout all my primary and secondary school years, I assumed that the wearing of cotton wool in that ear was the reason why I was having difficulty hearing lessons and also conversations, even when I was in smaller groups of people.

I remember being shouted at by the teacher in front of the whole class of pupils during a technical lesson in secondary school, because I hadn't complied with his instructions.

I felt so embarrassed and annoyed at that moment in time, and I really wanted to make him aware of how I felt, and that I did not deserve to be in receipt of that kind of public humiliation.

The truth was, though, that I was not aware that I should have been able to notify him that I was deaf in my left ear, as the result of a childhood operation during which my eardrum had been removed.

It wasn't until I was around the age of seventeen that the penny dropped, and I suddenly realised how naïve I had been; losing that eardrum had been the reason for my poor overall hearing, which had nothing to do with cotton wool affecting my ability to hear properly.

It was also the reason why I avoided being in groups of classmates. I could not properly converse with them, as I was unable to follow the flow of the conversations. I effectively chose to become a loner in order to avoid being classed as being weird because I couldn't interact with them, as I couldn't follow the dialogue well enough.

I can't help thinking how different my life might have been, if only my mother had explained to me that I'd had an operation; what had transpired during it; and what affect it was likely to have upon me throughout my life.

If I had known that I had been deprived of my hearing during that operation, I could have stood up to that teacher and made him, and the entire class, aware that I wasn't ignoring his teachings or deliberately being disruptive. I had a medical reason for my behaviour in that incident.

I could also have asked my classmates to maybe speak louder, or slower, to help me understand the dialogue in order to assist me to become part of the group.

The cost of not knowing my childhood medical history was that it caused me to needlessly withdraw from the company of friends or acquaintances, each of whom might have helped me to become a more outgoing and sociable person.

Such friends could have been beneficial to my sense of worth, character, and ability to grow into a well-balanced and confident individual: one who would not have felt the need to shy away from people or situations, which might actually have allowed such situations to become easier, and more manageable.

Although the operation was performed at a very young age, it is important to fast-forward through the years for you to understand its effect, year on year, upon my wellbeing and development (or otherwise).

My mother knew that operation had robbed me of hearing in my left ear, yet she never ever told me that I would have to carry that impediment with me for the rest of my life.

What a cruel and horrible way for her to send her youngest son out to face the world.

So much for there being a loving, caring family future to look forward to …

Little did I know, though, that a further operation had been performed on me, also at a very young age, which I was not told about at any time either, and which I would only discover and realise for myself in later years.

Returning to when I was still that young kid, the family circumstances changed, in that our dwelling house was now too small following the end of WW2, and the addition of twins to its family numbers in June 1947.

As new-born kids our cot wasn't a proper cot as such, but rather the unique use of one drawer within a chest of drawers.

I can only assume that this was the tried and tested cot method in use for each of my older siblings when they were born.

Our new abode was several miles away from the area in which we were born, and where our parents, grandparents, and siblings lived their lives prior to and during those war years.

This was a new-build area where every house had its own separate and private entrance door. Several styles of housing were being built, and ours was described as being "four-in-a-block".

Our family had been allocated a ground-floor flat, with a neighbour above in a very similar layout, although slightly modified as it had an internal stairway from its entrance door up to the main house level.

The other two houses within our block had the same layout as ours, only having been built in mirror image.

In comparison to our previous abode, this new house was huge.

Upon entering through the outer door there was a small square lobby where there was an internal glass door. This was a wooden frame door with four separate panes of glass.

Beyond that door was a long hallway, off which were three bedrooms, and at the end of that hallway was a door which led into the living area, featuring a bay window and a fireplace.

This was a coal-burning fireplace, with the coal storage area being within a further door from the hallway, close to the entrance door.

Surprisingly, an unexpected feature was that every bedroom also had its own fireplace. An early form of central heating, maybe. There were some drawbacks to these facilities though. Quite apart from the cost of burning all that coal were the potential health and safety issues. Parents regarded it as unsafe to have fires burning in bedrooms occupied only by kids, even older kids. Those facilities were not therefore fully utilised.

As you travelled down the hall and arrived at the living room door, the hall took a left turn to where you would find the entrance doors to the kitchen area, and to the bathroom, which had a full-sized bath, wash basin, and proper flushing toilet, and also enough room to move about.

More importantly, it was only for our own family use. No more folk banging on the W.C. door, or shouting to hurry up, from someone from a different household on the same landing as at the previous abode.

The kitchen was an almost square shape of decent size, with two large square ceramic sinks as a single unit. One of the sinks was much deeper than the other, which was presumably for clothes washing. There was also a built-in pantry cupboard, built-in display type units for dishes, etc., as well as another cupboard which housed an immersion-type water heater.

I know what you're thinking at this moment in time.

I had started writing about my earliest memory of life which I've not yet revealed, yet I've listed endless amounts of details of all manner of stuff which could be perceived as being memories.

Those particular memories were formed over a period of time after that which was regarded as my first memory. My maternal grandmother, sister, husband, and their only child were all still living on Argyle Street for several years after we had moved.

I think the reason for that was due to their dwelling not being overcrowded, and therefore they were far down the pecking order for rehousing.

Growing up, and being taken to visit them over the years, is where I gathered all the details and memories expressed in relation to our previous accommodation.

I have vivid memories of my granny and the unusual things she would say to me as she gave me tea and something to eat when I would visit. Such things as 'That'll put lead in your pencil', and 'This is for my wee cock in the corner.'

Although I didn't understand what she meant, I really did feel that such comments were entirely inappropriate for the ears of such a young boy as I.

I'm now very close to revealing that earliest memory, but I need to set the scene, in order for you to fully picture and understand the set-up which caused my fear and alarm at such a young and tender age.

The hallway ran through the centre of the house, with bedrooms off either side. As a result, the living room opened up to be entirely to the right of its entrance door. In the centre of the wall facing you, as you entered the room, there was quite a wide chimney breast with fireplace, and to the extreme right was a fairly wide bay window which formed a major part of the frontage of the building.

A large rectangular patterned carpet covered most of the floor and, as was the case in those days, linoleum covered the areas between the edges of the carpet and each of the walls.

The room was furnished with a three-piece suite, sideboard, folding dining table, and small black and white television, which could only receive the BBC channel.

My mother was part of the Ladies Committee of our local parish church, and they were tasked with raising funds for the upkeep of the church. They had to come up with ideas about what items they could make to be sold at church fetes, such as leather purses, and embroidered tablecloths of assorted sizes.

These were to be made in each committee member's own home and it was up to each person to decide how much time per week was allocated to the task.

One night in particular, I know not why, there was only my mother and me at home. She had just put more coal on the fire, which seemed to make the room darker by dimming out the light from the existing flames.

She was then concentrating on whatever she was making for the church fete, whilst she had left me sitting on the potty which was on the linoleum area in the corner of the room, facing towards the living room door, beyond which would be a view along the full length of the hallway to the external door.

In our house it was not referred to as a potty. It was just known as the "po".

Probably due to her knowledge that my young toilet habits were never rushed, she confidently just continued with her creativity.

Suddenly the house was in complete darkness, and I couldn't see a thing. I remember her saying, 'It's all right, I just need to put a shilling in the meter, just sit where you are.'

I could hear her rummaging through the coins in her purse, and then saying, 'I don't have a shilling. I'll need to ask Mrs C upstairs if she has a spare one.'

With that, she opened the living room door and

started walking up the dark hallway, towards the outside door. As she opened that door, there were feeble chinks of light from the street lighting, which silhouetted her as she left our home to go round to the rear of the building to knock on Mrs C's door.

Because of the street lighting, I could see that my mother had left the door wide open when she left, and knew that I had been left all alone in the dark, which seemed creepily quiet, and I felt so vulnerable.

What if she doesn't come back? I asked myself.

What if someone else comes into the house instead? I wondered and feared.

It seemed like forever before light was restored and my fears diminished.

In respect of my sitting on the po during that crisis, I think you could safely say, appropriately, 'Job done.'

That was the story I always recounted as being my earliest memory of life.

As mentioned previously, it was very scary at the time, but it is really just funny now.

At some point though, a new memory was recalled, which had to fall prior to the one just disclosed. This new memory means that it has actually now become my earliest memory of life.

There's no particular reason for me to remember this incident, except that it was to become a bit of an adventure for me.

Once again there was just my mother and me as we left our existing house in Argyle Street, Port Glasgow, and crossed the main road to board a bus to take us to see our new home.

Although I had seen buses passing by the end of our street, I had never been on one, so this was something to look forward to.

The buses were mostly red in colour, and my mother lifted me onto the platform at the rear. We sat in a seat on the lower deck, although a curved stairway led to the upper platform.

The seats were wooden-slatted throughout and were generally not very comfortable. The driver was alone within his own cabin, which was accessed by means of climbing into it from outside the front of the bus.

Passengers would enter or leave the bus from the rear platform but doing so could be fraught with danger as there were no doors on this platform.

The driver would take his instructions from the "clippie", who could be male or female, by using the company standard method of the ringing of the bell in his cabin. This could be one ring for stop, or two rings for go, for example.

After a mile or two, the driver veered right onto a route which would take us up a hill, which was called Clune Brae, towards the area where new housing estates were being built. This hill was quite steep, and we travelled slower and slower until we reached its summit.

Shortly after that, we encountered a feature which was a very large boulder by the side of the road, which was known as the Bogle Stone. As we passed that stone, the bus turned left because there was no new road created as yet to access the area the new house was in. We had to alight from the bus at that point and walk towards where we would find the new estate within which our new house could be found. That estate was called Boglestone.

Although many homes were still under construction, ours seemed to be almost complete, even though there was a joiner still carrying out some work in the kitchen as my mother perused our new abode.

As we arrived back at our existing home, there were many things about my adventure that day which I would remember for many years to come.

Having quickly settled into our new home it became a ritual that Saturday night was bath night for my sister and me.

It was always the case that the fire in the living room was backed up early so that there were plenty of flames to keep us warm, as we both were naked before the bath was ready.

A tin bath was positioned on the fireside rug and was then filled with soapy water of a suitable temperature for our tender skin.

My twin sister was always bathed first, then dried, and finally dressed in pyjamas, ready for bed. The same procedure then befell me, but prior to being put to bed, we had to drink our Ovaltine. Once in bed, a light was left on until we were fast asleep.

If you were able to imagine those scenes in your mind, there's no doubt you'd be thinking it was altogether a very nice, warm and loving family event.

A kind of Christmas-card type of scene which would bring a joyous and contented smile to your face.

What you wouldn't be able to see in that homely and lovely virtual picture though, was the pre-planned cruel and mental torture lying in wait for us, if either of us failed our mother's near-impossible test.

The rules of the test were disclosed to us before either of us went into the bath. She held a caramel sweetie in front of each of our faces, and this was our prize if we succeeded in following her rules. If either of us failed, we would get to watch the sweetie burn in the fire.

The actual test was quite simplistic. If we cried because soap went into our eyes whilst our hair was being washed, we failed the test.

During her bathing and hair washing, my sister hadn't cried, and whilst I was sitting in the bath, she enjoyed munching on her sweetie.

When it came to my turn, soap suds duly went into my eyes, and the stinging of the suds surely caused me to start crying. It also caused my mother to loudly start to scold me and to also roughly manhandle me during the drying process.

Having finished being bathed, dried, and having my PJs put on, my mother took hold of my left arm and pulled me closer towards the fire as she reminded me of what would happen if I cried. She once again held the sweetie in front of my face as she uttered the words, 'Now you can watch it burn,' as she threw it into the back of the fire.

She may have thought she'd taught me a lesson, and that I'd obey her forever more, but she didn't realise she had made a really huge mistake.

The mistake was one of giving me prior warning.

Even though I was just a toddler, somehow I had enough time and wherewithal to know how I was going to react if I failed her test.

I would show her no reaction, nor any more tears. No apologies, nor pleading with her to change her mind. Also, I wouldn't stare into the fire to watch it burn. I would just stare into her eyes, hoping she would get the message that I recognised that cruelty was in her blood. I wasn't sure if my sister would have suffered the same outcome had she also cried.

I already knew that my twin sister was a much more loved part of the family than I was. In fact, even at my young age, I was already aware that I felt no love towards me from anyone in the family, and for the most part I always felt largely ignored.

I think all members of the family might have been fed up and annoyed that I was always crying in comparison to my twin sister.

When young kids of the human species, as well as the animal species, suffer pain, their method of communicating such pain is by crying.

The longer it took to discover the source of the pain, and treat its cause, the longer would be the crying time. In my case the cause was mastoid infection of the left ear.

It's my belief that my constant crying caused the whole family, individually and collectively, to resent me for annoying their peace and quiet so often as I announced my pain.

That resentment of me, in my opinion, continued throughout my lifetime, even after my operation, recovery, and ongoing treatment became known to them as the cause of my "behaviour".

None of them seemed willing to acknowledge and/or accept that perhaps their resentment should have been replaced with a modicum of sympathy and/or forgiveness.

We never had a family pet, but I truly believe that, if we had had a dog, it would have received much more love, care, and attention than I ever did from any other family member.

I thought there was a possibility that this test would have been passed off as just a joke if my sister had cried, as my mother wouldn't want to punish the golden child.

My test could still proceed though, as there was no reason why I should be shown any form of leniency.

I had no idea that I was capable of such adult thinking and planning when I was just a very young kid. Somehow, I just knew that saying nothing was more powerful than showing any other kind of reaction.

I genuinely felt that this incident, and my response to it, was a fundamental seed in the creation of the character I would grow up to be. The strong silent type.

Somehow, from my very early days, I perceived the family to be a "gang" of which I was not part. When I felt bullied there was no-one I could turn to, so therefore I silently resented each and every one of them. On a daily basis, there was not one person who would show me any kind of love or want to play with me.

Ongoing weekly bath nights would add further seeds in my mind in relation to my future characteristics, although I didn't understand the meaning or reasoning relating to my astute observations of Bro.2's behaviour on those Saturday nights.

Week after week, on our bath nights, Bro.2 would always be sitting on the couch in the living room as the bathtub was being made ready for his young siblings, and he would stay there until we were both washed, dried, and in our jim-jams.

To put it another way, he stayed for the whole time whilst we were both naked, after which he then disappeared.

I had no idea why that would be the case, but at that time, it was something which just didn't seem to be right within my young and inquisitive mind.

Over time, the tin bath was no longer in use as we were both stretching in size a bit and were now being bathed together in the main bath. Bro.2 was therefore no longer able to observe the bath-time proceedings.

What also became more apparent to me was. that

most of the time, my siblings were never really anywhere around in the house. It seemed to be just mainly my mum and me.

I could understand that my older brothers would be at school, but I'd no idea where my sister was. There was never anyone around for me to play with, so I would often spend some time playing with my Dinky toys.

There was one time, though, when my mother had to go out somewhere and she arranged for Bro.2 to be in the house to look after me.

I would have been around four then, as I knew I hadn't yet started primary school, and that would have meant that Bro.2 was around ten. I'm not sure of the legality of that arrangement on an age basis, but in any event, since my father worked constant nightshifts, he was also on the premises, albeit sleeping in bed.

This was the first time I had a brother to play with, and he asked me to play a war game with him.

He was to be a film director and we both had to be the actors in this film where we were enemies.

His directions to me were to fall down on my back once I had been shot. I wouldn't die right away though, he told me. I would still have time to shoot him before I died, whereupon he would also fall down onto the floor.

Action time arrived and I duly followed his directions by shooting him as I fell backwards onto the floor to die.

He also fell onto the floor beside me, around about my knee level, and as he did this, his hand went up the leg of my baggy shorts and formed a fist around my then naked and flaccid penis.

I remember shouting 'Hey!' when that happened.

'It's OK,' he said. 'There's nothing to worry about.'

'Your hand is freezing,' I replied, but he said nothing.

I was aware by this point that I was now fully erect whilst he was still holding onto me, and that lasted for two or three minutes whilst we lay there motionless. I had no idea why that was happening or what was his reason or purpose for doing that.

He then got up, saying, 'I'll get you some juice and biscuits,' which he did, and he then disappeared into the bathroom.

None of us mentioned this again, but I didn't know why.

I guess I was trying to process in my mind if what had just happened was in any way related to all my memories of his presence during our tin-bath nights.

In any event, I generally felt somewhat confused by this, but also felt the need to trust that my brother would cause me no harm.

The following day there was only my mother and me around, with no sight of any siblings.

Whenever my mother found fault with me or was angry with me, she would skelp my bare bum, and if I cried, she would tell me in a loud voice, 'When you stop (crying), I'll stop (beating me).'

Throughout the various stages of growing up, there was always a question running through my mind. If this was a family, why did I never feel as if I was a part of it?

Soon enough it came time that I was due to start school, but I wasn't used to being in the company of other kids and was therefore very quiet and shy. Of course, I blamed this shyness entirely on the way I was raised within the family home, having been ignored by everyone.

I always had the impression that my siblings had been instructed to avoid being in my company by my mother because, to her, I was some kind of problematic upstart.

There was never a day throughout my childhood that I felt any feeling of love towards me from anyone within the family.

She was forever finding fault with me and treating me as if I was deliberately trying to cause her problems. She would be shouting at me, calling me names, and bringing me down in front of people. These things seemed to be always high on her agenda.

Even if there was no truth to what she was saying, she knew she was making me look bad because she didn't have to provide any evidence to support what she was saying.

An example of the kind of stuff she would say about me was the time when she shouted at me from the kitchen, at the top of her voice, 'You're not cleaning yourself properly after using the toilet. That's disgusting and downright filthy. You need to sort yourself out from now on.'

'If I have to tell you this again, I'll beat you black and blue.'

It didn't matter to her whereabouts I was in the house, she wanted everyone to hear how she degraded me.

Anyone hearing her words would quickly form their own opinion about the kind of toe-rag person I was and would most definitely want to avoid being in my company.

Quite clearly her hatred of me was blatantly obvious.

If there was any love or compassion towards me, she could have called on me, or come to me, and quietly whispered in my ear to advise me what she thought was something which I needed to pay more attention to, and perhaps even have shown me, by way of evidence.

On a daily basis the gap between my family and me was forever widening to the point where I just opted to live a solitary life as some kind of lodger, who was also expected to be a live-in slave for dishwashing, tea-making, and other menial tasks, whilst my siblings had a much easier home life.

I was quite prepared to live this kind of life as a "strong and silent" person, in the knowledge and comfort that I had no feelings for any single person who was supposedly a family member of mine.

I knowingly made this decision, which would last throughout my life, even though I was fully aware that currently I was only around seven years of age.

Education was what I would focus on to ensure that I was able to progress through life without having to rely on any of them to support me beyond the normal schooling cycle.

I still had no real friends in primary school but there were one or two people with whom I could have the odd few words.

One day in particular, my desk-mate Danny surprised me with a request. We were sitting at our usual desk at the very back of the classroom when he whispered to me, 'I'll show you mine if you show me yours.'

At that point, he pulled up the leg of his shorts and pulled out his flaccid penis to show me.

It was not going to be possible for me to pull up the leg of my shorts though, as I was already past the point of still being flaccid. I had to undo the buttons on my flies and take it out that way, but I put it away very quickly again.

This was the second time in my young life that

another boy showed interest in my penis, and the second time that I had become instantly aroused.

I didn't understand why that should be the case, nor could I understand why I didn't feel embarrassed by it, even though I was effectively still a very quiet, timid, and shy young boy.

I realised then that that kind of behaviour wasn't just confined to within my own family and seemed to be just something that some young boys do which was generally accepted as having inquisitive or educational value but was conducted in private by two consenting boys of similar ages.

Danny and I never did anything like that again, nor was it ever mentioned between us. Life and education just carried on.

At home, my mother was still her usual self, finding ways to try to humiliate me.

The latest thing happened one night when I was aged eight, and having a bath. I'm assuming she was listening outside of the locked bathroom door and couldn't hear any water being splashed about by me in the bath.

She probably had her own thoughts about what I might have been up to and wanted to catch me doing it.

Suddenly the bathroom door flew wide open because the door lock had given way under her pressure, meaning she then had forcibly violated my right of privacy.

What she found was that I was still fully clothed, and balancing on the rim of the bath, trying to make my way from one end of the bath to the other, as if I was walking along a tightrope, whilst trying not to fall into, or off, the bath.

There was nothing she said which resembled anything like any kind of apology for wilfully, culpably, and aggressively breaching my right to privacy, as a minor within what should have been a place of sanctuary for me, and where I should be protected from any form of potential harm likely to befall me, even if that harm might potentially befall me from the hands of that very person who was meant to be my protector.

The actual words which she shouted at me were along the lines of, 'What stupid stunt is this you're up to? You're supposed to be in here for a bath, not for playing daft games. Get your bath done, get your pyjamas on and get to bed. There's no supper for you tonight.'

Once again, her actions, and the level of her voice, ensured that everyone knew that I was still being the bad boy and giving her grief again, only this time she managed to deprive me of sustenance as well, by way of an extra and needless punishment.

So far I've not mentioned ever being out to play when it was not a school day. From age four I was sent out to play, but all the other kids were at school. After I started school until around age eight, I was allowed out as well, but mainly during school holidays, when I was wearing white T-shirt, shorts, socks, and newly whitened sandshoes. I'm pretty sure she just wanted me out of the house as I was sent out at 8am every day. No other kids were out at that time, and I just looked like a lost soul wandering around aimlessly as I just toyed with the breeze.

My playtimes stopped at around age nine. Other kids were out playing football, but I was regarded as the enemy by them because my mother was always shouting at them to go somewhere else to play. She didn't want any of her windows broken whilst they played on the grassy area across the road from her house. She was relentless in chasing them away, and they would keep returning every now and again. And so it went on.

I don't know why but I was not allowed to open the door to anyone who knocked on it. My sister opened the door to a boy I knew from school, who might have hoped I would go out to play with him on that day. He was not a friend of mine, but maybe was hoping to become a friend. He would have walked several miles to arrive at my address, full of joy, hope, and optimism, that someone he liked might like him also, and be willing to become a pal.

What he expected to happen was unbelievably nowhere near what actually transpired when my sister opened the door to him on that fateful morning.

Without warning she started shouting at him, telling him to go away and to never come back again to this door, adding what would be the consequences if he ever returned, as she slammed the door in his face.

This boy had done nothing wrong. He deserved none of that kind of treatment. All of a sudden, his optimism had been destroyed and he left the property, probably in fear, alarm, and tears as he headed back the miles to his own home, lonely and with no-one to comfort and support him throughout his traumatic return journey.

My sister couldn't have cared less about the mental anguish she caused that young, innocent boy to suffer, suddenly, unexpectedly, and without warning at that moment in time, nor what length of time it would take for him to recover, or even if he ever would recover.

That morning he had left his home full of the joys of spring, in the hope that his future could be about to become brighter as he might form a new friendship, and it ended with him possibly needing years of therapy to overcome the effects of the treatment imposed upon him by my horrible, disgusting, bully of a sister.

I felt real sorrow and deep shame due to the treatment he suffered, simply because he felt the desire to seek to become a friend of mine. Contact between us never occurred thereafter.

There was a time later on when my left ear became a bit problematic and I was taken to Greenock Ear, Nose, and Throat hospital and was admitted for three days just for observation. During this stay I was to realise just how naïve I still was.

The ward was quite long but there were only half a dozen beds occupied. In those days it was quite common for patients to be admitted for observation only.

An older boy was admitted not long after me, and he really seemed to be very confident and sure of himself in my opinion, whereas I was still my usual timid and shy self.

He was allocated the bed opposite me and soon returned from the toilet in his pyjamas. He sat on the bottom corner of his bed where he intentionally sat at forty-five degrees, so that he would be able to talk to, and look at, every other patient as he introduced himself.

He said his name was John and he was a fifteen-year-old singer. He was in for five days for observation as his throat was extremely sore and he had to rest it.

Just then a passing nurse told him to take his situation seriously and rest his throat, otherwise he might not get back to singing. He continued sitting there and began looking through a music magazine.

Having never read a music magazine, I was trying to read some of the larger typeface on the back cover, which was facing towards me, by leaning my head over to the right to align my sight with the typeface. All of a sudden, my attention was diverted elsewhere.

He must have been wearing a brand-new pair of pyjamas which were well starched. As a result of the way he was sitting, the pyjama flies were wide open with the left side raised up and the other side somewhat folded down.

The whole of his flaccid penis was clearly visible just lying there in clear view, but only to me, due to the relative angles of our postures.

I noticed that he had a fair amount of long pointy skin at the end of it, and that it was different from mine. I began to wonder if there was something wrong with me.

I quietly shouted, 'John,' and when he looked over at me I discreetly signalled to him to cover himself up so as not to be embarrassed.

I noticed quite often as time went on that he couldn't manage to keep quiet for any length of time, which would make his observation period pretty useless.

Prior to my lying down for the night, I went to the toilet, taking with me two strips of Elastoplast as I was concerned about not being like John.

I stretched my skin forward and held it in place with the Elastoplast and would check it in the morning.

A nurse woke me up next morning and asked how I was feeling, to which I replied, 'Fine.' She then asked if my bowels had moved.

I shrugged my shoulders to let her know I didn't understand her question.

She threw her eyes towards the roof in disbelief and then asked if I'd been to the toilet, to which I firmly said, 'No.'

That was a phrase I'd never heard before, so her eye gesture was wholly inappropriate. She could have been more understanding and helpful.

Also, she knew she had just awakened me, therefore there was no need to ask the question at all, as obviously I'd not been anywhere.

I checked the Elastoplast after she left, and my skin had returned to where it had always been.

So here I was again; still showing the level of my naïvety.

On returning home, I realised that I'd had another childhood operation which my mother hadn't told me about, and which I was not aware of. I did not know or understand why it was necessary to have such an operation and why my mother, once again, felt that I was not entitled to know what alterations she had consented to and allowed to happen to my body without my knowledge or consent. Not even after the fact.

This other operation was called a circumcision, and now, at nine years of age, I realised that this medical adjustment to my anatomy, discovered accidentally, due to my passing acquaintance with John the singer, following my brief observational stay in hospital, was once again an unspoken-of intervention within my medical tissues, at the behest of my mother.

I'm of the thought that it would have suited her better to pay more attention to looking after my heart, mind, and soul, and to be the seat of my learning, as opposed to the leathering of my seat.

It would be not long after my tenth birthday when my life seemed to develop more freedom, to be able to choose to do the things I wanted to do, but that only followed on from having been enrolled into the parish's recently formed Boy Scout troop by my mother.

At that time, it was also noticeable that there was decidedly less hassle towards me from her as well. Perhaps she felt that I needed to be in a more disciplined environment and would become less of a problem child due to being enrolled within such a structured unit as the Scouts.

From my viewpoint, though, for the first time in my life, I was amongst so many other boys of a similar age to me, as opposed to being so desperately alone at home, that I became very appreciative of this culture. I was of course still that shy and timid boy, but the fact that I was part of a set routine of Friday night interactions, of learning so many new things, like knots and their uses, about trees, birds, and nature, that I grew to be more confident within myself, and possibly began to feel less shy.

Going camping, singing around the campfire, marching around the town in parades and other such activities were all great confidence builders for me.

Meanwhile, at home, I remained that lonely, timid, and shy boy who was still the runt of the family.

Up until now I had never mentioned what the family sleeping arrangements were, but that information is essential to the direction of the story going forward.

My two older brothers slept in their own single beds in what was known as the "bottom room".

My mother and my twin sister shared a double bed in the "middle room", as they were the only female members of the family.

As my father always worked nightshift, he would sleep in the double bed in the "back room" during the day, whilst it would be my bed throughout the night.

After I had gone to bed one night, Bro.2 came into my room and told me he would be sleeping in the bed with me, but never gave a reason why that was to be the case.

At age sixteen, he was way bigger and heavier than me, whilst, by comparison, I was a very feeble ten-year-old.

He told me that he wanted me to do something for him but said I must promise him that I would not tell my mum about it.

Although I didn't know what he wanted, I said, 'OK.' But he repeated it again, that I must promise. I agreed.

He then took hold of my right hand and closed it into a fist around his erect penis, with his own hand around my hand, keeping my hand in place. He then silently started making my hand move up and down his penis whilst I had no idea what was going on.

Due to the build of him, and my feeble frame, I felt that I had no option other than to do what I was told.

After a short while, he told me to keep going, 'Until I tell you to stop,' as he removed his hand from being on top of mine.

None of this meant anything to me, as I didn't know the reason or purpose for what was occurring.

Then, as had happened all those years ago, his hand was now once again around my penis, which was again in an erect state. Instead of just holding it as he had previously, he started to manipulate it in the same way in which he had me manipulating him.

No words were being spoken as these events were

unfolding. I suddenly felt my body stiffening up and then quickly relaxing again, and at that point, I stopped manipulating him.

'Did you enjoy that?' he asked. I told him that I just wanted him to stop. 'Did you not like it?' he quizzed. My response was the same as before, and I turned somewhat angrily onto my side and fell asleep.

Next day I somehow thought no more about it. I don't know if I was trying to blot it out of my mind. It was something which I felt ashamed of, and for which there seemed to be no reason. I had no understanding of what that was all about.

That night, as I went into the room to go to bed, Bro.2 was already in my bed. He never spoke and neither did I. During the first five minutes which passed, and whilst we both silently lay there, I became already erect, but I knew not why.

The bedclothes were then thrown down the bed to around knee level, by my brother. Again, he had taken hold of my right hand, but his plan was different this time as he closed my hand around my own penis, with his hand on top of mine, as he started the manipulation. During this he was using his left hand on himself.

He told me to continue to manipulate myself as he took his hand off my hand, and he seemed to just want to watch me.

Again, I felt that I had no option but to do as I was told.

It came to the point where the outcome, questions, and answers were all just repeated from the previous night, then I slept.

As I woke up next morning, I was aware of immense feelings of shame; of guilt; also of disgust.

Those feelings were because of the part I had played in the events which had transpired over the previous two nights.

I also had feelings of extreme anger and hatred towards my brother, because he had coerced me into performing actions which I couldn't begin to understand. I felt that, in some way, I had been abused by him, yet I had no physical bruises. My mind was the area in which I felt most troubled and damaged, though.

The thoughts in my head included memories going back to my tin-bath days, when he was always there before, during, and after having been bathed, when I was that naked young kid, every Saturday night.

I also remembered the time when he was holding my penis during his "army game" when I was around four.

I had no awareness that the penis could serve any other purpose than to allow the emptying of the bladder. It had no other function that I was aware of.

Although I had known, for all my life, of the many occasions when variations between being flaccid or erect would occur, there was no known reason or understanding on my part of why that would happen.

I thought long and hard about what actions I should be invoking following my brother's abuse of me, but it was a relatively easy decision for me to make.

Having always been the runt of the family, I was the one who was always ignored by them all. He was now the one who would be seen to be persona non grata. I would ensure that the whole family would recognise his disgrace at my hands, whilst he worried about when I might break my promise not to tell my mother.

Less than a week later, it was a Sunday morning, and

the family had gone to chapel to celebrate Mass. It wasn't the whole family though, as my father worked overtime during the day on Sundays but worked only nights during the week.

I wasn't at church either but couldn't remember why. In order to pass my time until their return, I decided to borrow Bro.2's pack of cards to see how high I could build a card tower.

I knew he kept them in the drawer in his room, so I wouldn't have to ask him for them. He was at church anyway.

There seemed to be a lot of junk in his drawer, so it was taking a while to find them.

All of a sudden I realised that I had been grabbed around my waist from behind and felt that I was being tickled by someone who could only be Bro.1, who I didn't know was at home and thought was still in bed.

As he fell onto his back upon the bed, he dragged me with him whilst still having his arms around my waist. It became a mixture of tickling and wrestling he was engaging in. I was still in my pyjamas, and at some point he managed to turn me over onto my back and he was lying on top of me with a fair amount of bodily movement taking place.

At this point I was shocked to realise that he was completely naked, and I could feel his hands were all over my body.

My pyjama bottoms were around my ankles now, and his mouth was around my penis.

He was trying to push his finger into my bum whilst he was also trying to push my knees and legs up towards my shoulders. Having succeed with that manoeuvre, he then changed from using his finger to trying to push his penis into my bum.

At some point within his various actions, he had also been trying to force my penis into him as well, both orally and anally.

It has to be remembered that he was twenty years old, twice my age, and I was entirely helpless to resist his attack.

Having released me, he seemed to be cleaning up, and that was my opportunity to escape and lock myself into the bathroom, where I stayed until the "blessed ones" returned from church.

Whilst I hid in there, I thought it was unbelievable that such an attack was even a possibility between two human beings, let alone two brothers of the same household of such differing ages.

How did both of my brothers manage to acquire their knowledge of such matters?

Did they conspire with each other to "educate" me by abusing me in the same manner?

What they each did to me was horrific, barbaric, traumatic, and also Illegal!

They both were predators and child abusers!

This was not going to remain a secret. My plans were to wait until the time was right, when only my mother and I were alone in the house, and then I would make her aware of everything her beloved two oldest sons had inflicted upon me. The promise I had made to Bro.2 was now null and void.

Two days later, the time had come for the mother to hear the most horrific and unbelievable story imaginable, direct from the mouth of her youngest and most innocent son, who was only ten years old.

We stood in the hallway outside the living room door as I recounted to her every single tiny detail, concerning every part of my body, that each of my brothers had defiled and interfered with, throughout all of their abusive behaviour carried out against my will.

She would have heard the full details which I was telling her, knowing full well that I wasn't capable of understanding many of the words or descriptions which I was using, as there had never been any kind of discussion or instruction which would have breached the barrier beyond the level of my childhood innocence.

That would have become even more clear with the story's ending, when I said, 'Bro.1 was playing with his own penis, and then string came out of it.'

She stood there briefly and quietly, for what seemed like only a minute; thereafter she just turned her back to me. She never said a word or asked any questions as she entered the living room and closed the door, leaving me standing there in the empty hall, feeling alone, abandoned, disbelieved, and still the runt of the family, whose life had no meaning.

Quite clearly, she would be taking no action against her oldest sons. Perhaps she was the one who instructed them to educate me into the ways of "adult life".

I put on my jacket and left the house as I went for a walk in the direction of the Mill Dam.

If she was watching me through the living room window, she would have realised where I was heading.

Knowing the circumstances of my leaving there should have been alarm bells loudly ringing in her head at that point.

Kids had drowned there in previous years, and I had just suffered a series of traumatic sexual abuse attacks at the hands of her adult sons. If my mother didn't believe me when I told her my version of events, she had a sin to answer for. She chose to ignore me, instead of being the one person who should have comforted me.

The mother who was surely watching me walking away, and who couldn't be sure that I would ever return. The mother who should be dreading the police knocking on her door with fatal news about her youngest son's tragic suicidal death by drowning.

The mother who should hang her head in shame for her treatment of this son, and who should no longer be licking the altar rails, taking Holy Communion, and pretending to be a good Catholic mother.

Clearly, she would have been untruthful during her confessions for not admitting her liability in the cover-up of my abuse.

I was still a shy and timid ten-year-old boy, the unloved runt of the family, whose fragile young body had been ravaged by each of his two adult brothers in turn, to satisfy their own personal levels of satisfaction, whilst having been admonished for their crimes by the same matriarch who bestowed the "family runt" accolade upon my soul from the day of my birth. An accolade which she perpetuated continuously even until that moment.

During my walk, there were many things I needed to think about, and many questions I needed to ask myself, including where I would place myself from now on within this family, if indeed anywhere.

As with any academic subjects, the older you become, the more you are expected to learn and to retain within your memory banks. During exams you must recall such relevant knowledge from memory, in order to pass the exams and achieve good qualifications to be able to secure a better future for yourself.

Thinking of recent incidents with my brothers, who were clearly quite older than me, it stands to reason that they knew stuff that I had no need to know at my age. They obviously knew about sexual matters which were way beyond my comprehension for my years, but I presume, for whatever reason, they thought they would teach me about such things prior to the point where I might need to have such knowledge.

I'm not sure whether their actions were for my education, or for their own sexual satisfaction. Their method of education though, leads me to the conclusion that they both had used and abused me for their own pleasure.

That being the case, and having thought about it, my final thoughts about each of my brothers was of *hatred* towards them both. My circumstances might dictate that I needed to continue to live in the same building as them for now, but they each now ceased to exist in my eyes from that moment on.

I have no idea if there is a genuine method for innocent young boys to properly gain knowledge of matters relating to sex, but whilst I was telling my mother about my issues with my brothers' abuse of me, this still shy, timid, and innocent kid felt really uncomfortable whilst describing the various activities which had been taking place.

I felt I was admitting to actions which I had been committing which I wouldn't want anyone else except myself to know about.

My mother now knew that I was actively capable of having a sex life, on my own or with others. That's a very onerous thought for a ten-year-old boy.

She was also aware that my sexual capability, due to the acts of my brothers, included my ability to engage in sex with other males. The female gender was never part of this "education".

I had considered talking to the police about my abuse but concluded that would be fraught with danger. For the first part, the family were capable of using gang culture and concocting a story proving I was just a lying troublemaker, and secondly they could throw me out of the house, or disown me, leaving me nowhere to live, or any money to live on.

They were seriously capable of either of those plans.

My decision would be to just live as a shadow within that house and use the Scouts as my support group and lifeline. I also needed to prepare myself for my 11 Plus exam and be ready for moving on to secondary school, which meant having to manage my "ear" situation all over again as I encountered new school pals.

purgatory;

I have to formally state for the record my feeling of new-found strength and freedom within this new, controlled-by-me regime.

I was feeling more strength and confidence also, as each week of attending the Scouts transpired. It began to feel like this was my family, unlike anything publicly portrayed as family in the arena of friends and extended family.

I think the Scout leaders were able to see an improvement in my skills and confidence as well, as I was approached to see if I was willing to help out at a Cub Scout beach outing the following weekend.

I jumped at the chance to gain experience at such an event, even though it was still just for our own parish Cubs.

There were limits as to the things I was capable of doing, as I was not qualified to supervise Cubs playing in the water, for example, but I was able to command distribution of meals when they were ready.

One young Cub was smart enough to spot a time when I was free and asked me to "swing" him. He explained his dad would do this for him at home sometimes. I told him he would need to explain it to me.

He said I would have to hold him tightly with one hand around each of his wrists, then I would have to spin myself round and round. He would be flying round in the air in circles, until I stopped spinning.

He loved it and wanted me to keep going all day. Thankfully for me, but sadly for him, the meals were ready, and I had work to do.

It was a great experience to take part in that event, even just watching all the other things that had been organised for that day and seeing the joy on all those young faces. I was thinking to myself that I would enjoy having the ability to acquire such organisational skills for the future.

As the weeks and months passed, I was living in a much stronger phase of my life within the house and was aware of potential changes shaping up. Engagements had taken place and plans were being formed for marriages to take place in around a year or so. Whilst I would celebrate those brothers moving out, I would take no part in any of their ceremonials.

How either of those men could have the gall to exchange vows with their "beloveds", considering their past behaviours, defied all logic in my mind.

Further to that, what plans did they have for any kids they might bring into this world, bearing in mind the crimes they perpetrated against their own ten-year-old innocent young brother, whilst each of them was a fully grown adult?

Would they be likely to transgress against their own young sons? Would they be likely to punish anyone else who might do so?

What hypocritical people they would be to punish someone for sexually abusing their son(s), given their own backgrounds.

I'm sure their fiancées would run like hell if they knew they were marrying child-molesting criminals!

Life within the Scouts was improving for me as I had been promoted to being a Patrol Leader and was also one of the three nominated flag bearers for parades.

I had also passed my 11 Plus exam and qualified to attend Saint Columba's Secondary School in Greenock.

Living a parallel life to me was my twin sister, but we had nothing in common. She was the "golden child" and was the only one who was important to my father. She mattered also to my mother, who also had a soft spot for Bro.2.

What a disaster for the parents, though, as she failed to qualify for the same school as me. She only qualified for Saint Stephens Secondary in Port Glasgow, which was a slightly less prestigious school.

They immediately set about having this "mistake" corrected as my sister should have qualified along with me. The school board disagreed, stating the correct decision had been reached.

The parents then contacted the local paper, *The Greenock Telegraph*, to try to drum up local support and have the original decision overturned.

Looking at the situation through my eyes, I could only assess that the more the parents kicked up a stooshie, the more my sister was being needlessly publicly embarrassed, and made a fool of, throughout the whole of the local community. What a red face the parents were creating for her.

I cannot definitely confirm that it was under discussion by the parents, but I believe an exchange might have been suggested by the parents to the school board that my sister and I should just swap schools.

The matter ended as originally decided, with even the parents losing face. The story slid away quietly into the background with me being the upstart again in my mother's eyes.

When I attended the Scouts on the Friday night of that week, one of the Troop Leaders brought a new recruit to join my patrol.

It was someone who was moving up to the Scouts from the Cub Scouts, as he was now of age for promotion.

I remembered his face from months ago as being the boy who asked me to swing him round during that Cub Scout day out.

He had a happy-looking face and a broad grin as he was introduced to me, and it was only at that point I realised that I never knew his name back then. He became the eighth member of the Otter Patrol that night and was introduced to the rest of the boys as Billy.

I really felt more in control in the house and was now twelve. There were some strange things happening though, which I couldn't understand. It was generally odd feelings more than anything else. There was one night when I had a strange dream about playing in the playground of my previous school. There was a shelter made of corrugated tin in which the pupils would take refuge in the rain.

In my dream there was a very high wind but there was no rain. Somehow, I was lying on top of that shelter being blown back and forward across the corrugated ridges. All of a sudden, I woke up to the sound of me moaning, with a feeling of wetness around my erect penis.

Although I was familiar with that feeling because of the issues concerning the attentions of my brothers, being wet there was an entirely new concept for me.

I found out that this was something called a wet dream, caused by puberty, which I knew nothing about. I had no warning that any of this could, or would, take place.

I'm guessing my brothers were showing more interest in me, hoping that they might entice that kind of reaction during their abusive behaviours with me, as they knew that I would be reaching puberty sometime soon.

I could begin to understand those odd feelings now. This boy was beginning to travel the route towards becoming a man.

A new phase of my life was about to happen, and as well as having to concentrate on improving my education, I also had a lot to learn about life and growing up.

One night at the Scouts, I was inspecting my patrol when something totally unexpected happened.

During my uniform inspection, and inspecting Billy's uniform, which, to be honest, was always immaculate, he said something which shook me to the core.

'I adore the ground you walk on!' he stated, smiling broadly.

My eyes popped out of my head, and my jaw almost hit the floor upon hearing that statement. I was speechless. No-one had ever intimated any kind feelings towards me at any point in my life.

He looked very pleased with himself that he had found the courage to make what seemed like a confession to me.

I kind of stuttered a response to him and I don't think I even said anything which made any kind of sense.

He had no idea how special his comment had made me feel. I had to stifle a tear knowing that there was now one person on this planet who appreciated my existence.

Each week after that, I ensured that I acknowledged him with some general, but friendly, passing comment.

There was a parade arranged within the chapel where the Papal Flag was to be dedicated, and all three of our flags were carried right up to the altar rails. The rest of the Scout troop followed the flagbearers up the aisle and took up the reserved pews at the head of the church, with the rest of the parishioners seated further back.

At the part of the ceremony where the dedication was to take place, the priest had to come off the altar, along with an altar boy who was carrying holy water, and another altar boy who was carrying incense.

I was the bearer carrying the Papal Flag, and the incense-carrying altar boy was Billy, who was allowed to perform that function instead of attending as a Boy Scout.

This was a very solemn occasion, so I have no idea how it came about that Billy and I could not stop laughing (discreetly) every time we looked at each other during that process.

We became good friends, even outside of the Scouts. Soon after that, Billy also attended the same school as me and would sit beside me on the school bus.

The set-up for classes in each of the first three years was based on the pupil's individual scores which had brought them to St Columba's High School.

If you were amongst the highest-scoring pupils, you would be allocated to class 1L, the ideology being that these pupils would be more likely to become lawyers or physicians, for example, and therefore would need to study Latin.

Using the same logic, the next level below those pupils would need to study science, and so were allocated to class 1S, as they might be scientists or similar, whilst the next group would be in class 1T with a view to becoming technicians or mechanics, for example.

When I first arrived there, I had been allocated to class 1S but was now about to enter class 3S.

On the first day of attending his new school, Billy found me in the playground at the morning break to tell me he had learned his first words of Latin. (I can't guarantee its accuracy).

'Amo, Amas, Amata. – I love, You love, We love,' he said proudly.

Having heard his Latin/English translation, my first thought was, *is he likely to be referring to us?*

Initially we would speak to one other on the phone each evening after school. There was no phone in our house, but there was a phone box about five minutes away and I would arrive there with a handful of 2p coins. His father was a businessman, so there was a house phone, and we would alternate the days when we would call each other.

As the days went on, the phone calls changed into me visiting his home, and being welcomed by his parents. I was accepted into that house as if I was part of the family. What a difference to be in a loving household each evening, instead of an isolation block in which I felt like a solitary prisoner.

Billy and I did many activities together including fishing, camping, hiking, and many others, but most Saturday nights we would be at church for confession in readiness for Mass and Communion on Sunday morning, where I would go to whichever Mass he was serving on, and then wait till he came outside, and we would talk for a while before parting ways.

There had been a realisation for quite a while, on my part, that I had very strong feelings for Billy. He was two years younger than me, but I was resolute in my own mind that I would never lay a finger on him. I never wanted him to feel the kind of hatred towards me that I felt towards my abusive brothers.

For all our nights away camping, I never wavered from my commitment to make sure he remained chaste.

There was one night, after I had put out the fire, when I went into the tent where Billy was laying out both of our sleeping bags, to find he had zipped both of them together into a double.

I wasn't sure if maybe he felt colder that night. We did sleep in the double although I kept my distance from him.

Another time when we were camping, the rain was really non-stop, and Billy's father came to fetch us from our solitary camping place. He took us to his own house and organised that we would both sleep in Billy's bed.

I have to be honest here, I'm not sure what his father's mindset was at that point. Billy and I had been in each other's company for about two years, almost constantly. He had no hesitation in allowing us to sleep together in the same double bed, in his house. Puberty was highly active within our teenage bodies, I would imagine, yet it was not discussed between us. We weren't "hands-on" with each other either, meaning we wouldn't put our arms around each other's back or shoulders.

Within his mind, was he accepting of whatever he

thought our relationship was, or was he totally trusting of our chastity?

I was now passionately in love with his son, and if my childhood had not been blighted by those brothers, then there is no doubt that a relationship might have formed between us. But I'm not sure if there was indeed any possibility of that.

I had stayed on into fourth year in school but was beginning to think I had made the wrong choice. I would be thinking more about that in the coming weeks.

Our Saturday night ritual of being at church involved us in having our usual walk afterwards to where Billy and I would part company for the night.

From there Billy had a short journey to his home, down Barr's Brae.

Prior to that, as I mentioned before, we went to confession, where the script between the priest and myself was usually as follows.

'Bless me, Father, for I have sinned. It's been one week since my last confession. I have said a few bad words, have lost my temper and pushed someone because I was angry,' I confessed.

'God bless you, my child. For your penance say five Our Fathers and ten Hail Marys. Go in peace,' the priest declared.

It's probably not the right thing to do, to make up sins instead of telling the truth because the real sins were far worse.

If I was to go to confession now, I would have to say, being truthful, 'It's been forty years since my last confession.'

I had thought about my school dilemma and told my mother one day, when I returned to the house after school, that I was leaving school.

When my father got out of bed to have his dinner and to get ready for his nightshift, he came into the living room where my mother and I both happened to be.

My mother told him that I had decided that I was leaving school.

It should be noted at this point that I was now seventeen years old, and my father had never, at any point in my life, said one word to me. Not ever.

This was an opportunity for him to speak that first word to me now!

Looking away from me, and towards his wife, he responded to the news he had just been given.

'It's about time he was bringing money into this house!' he said to her, as he left the room, still not uttering one word to me.

He was born in the Newcastle area, and I know from hearing him talking about me many times before, that he couldn't even say my name properly. Instead of calling me Hugh, he could only call me Shoo.

I had told Billy that I would be leaving school and looking for a job sometime soon, but hopefully it shouldn't change things too much between us.

We had our Saturday night walk home as usual, but it ended differently this time. We were at the crossroads where Billy would head down Barr's Brae.

He asked me to walk partly up Mill Dam Road, which was a country road with little traffic of any kind.

We stopped just after the first bend to the left, where he asked me if I could show him how to hold a girl if he was going to kiss her.

I put my left arm around his waist and pulled him closer to me, then my right hand went to the centre of his back where I pulled him even closer to me.

He then duplicated my movements, and our faces were really close. Our lips were about an inch apart, and we were staring into each other's eyes; we were also holding each other tightly.

My heart was pounding passionately, and I desperately wanted to kiss him. This was the biggest challenge ever for me to keep him chaste, and to prevent him from hating me.

I then moved my hands onto his arms, just below his shoulders, as I gently pushed him away, and told him to be careful going home, and that I'd see him at Mass next day.

My heart continued pounding all the way back to the house, as I relived those moments over and over.

As I lay there in bed thinking of that situation again, I suddenly had the most dreadful realisation imaginable, and I cried and cried for hours.

Those bloody brothers had messed up my mind more than I realised was even possible.

Billy was the one who had organised that scenario, and I was so busy trying to protect him from me taking advantage of him, that I failed to realise that I had not thought about what it was that he wanted.

I was the one who was so desperate to kiss him, and trying so hard not to, that it never occurred to me that Billy might have matured and possibly developed feelings for me. He had created a situation where he might have hoped that I would take the initiative as he was desperate for us to kiss, but he didn't have the courage himself to take it further.

As he walked down that road, he might have been desperately sad and disappointed that I had seemed to reject him. He probably hated me at that point because he was confident and sure that I had feelings for him.

This would have been the very *hatred* of me which I had spent so much time trying to avoid, but for the wrong reason.

With my having left school and now working long hours plus overtime, we gradually drifted apart and just lost contact with each other.

The aftermath of my brothers' abuse of me meant that Billy and I could had been deprived of the possibility of a life of beautiful love together.

Neither of us had been brave enough to push the boundaries or to talk about our own feelings for each other.

I guess I was still a quiet and shy boy, even then.

There were opportunities which could have led to a more satisfactory and joyful outcome though.

Whilst we held each other in that embrace, with our lips so close, Billy could have taken his original request a step further by asking, 'Will you please now show me how to kiss her?'

Without a doubt I wouldn't have hesitated and would have kissed him, because he had asked me to. I wouldn't have been taking advantage of him nor abusing him in those circumstances.

Alternately, I could have asked him, 'Do you know how to kiss her?' or 'Do you want me to show you how to kiss her?'

It would have been a free choice for him to make, and therefore we would have been making a decision based upon our passionate feelings for each other, whilst in that embrace, and whilst our lips were so close.

We could have sealed it with a kiss and belonged to each other, instead of that misunderstanding which needlessly tore us apart for life.

Although Billy and I had spent a lot of time

together, we had very little physical contact with each other; also there was never any dialogue concerning matters relating to puberty or any other kind of sexual context.

Referring to the way my brothers "educated" me in matters of sex, if they had told me that they wanted to talk to me about some changes which would be occurring within my body shortly, that would have taught me that sex was a subject which was OK to be talked about.

I would then have known how to raise the issue of sex with Billy.

We both were shy about discussing such topics, or unable to think of a way to broach sexual conversations.

Had we overcome such difficulties, then perhaps physical contact between us may have developed following dialogue.

My education from my brothers was by physical contact only, without any form of discussion about it.

Having left school and started to look for employment, I had an idea of what kind of job I wanted to do.

I had O Level passes in Mathematics, Mechanics, English, Technical Drawing, Art, and Woodwork, but what I enjoyed doing most of all was Technical Drawing. On that basis, I wanted to become a draughtsman.

There were opportunities locally within Scott Lithgow's, who were shipbuilders, and John G Kincaid & Co. Ltd., who built ships' engines.

I had arranged my first interview at Scott Lithgow's, and was told upon arrival that there were two applicants for interview.

I would be interviewed first and was told that I would need to wait until the other boy, from Greenock Academy, had his interview after me.

It was common knowledge that Academy pupils were more likely to succeed ahead of any pupil from any other school, so even before being interviewed, I knew what the outcome was likely to be.

It was not that the Academy had better teachers, it was just that the pupils' parents were the elite of the district, and they all had contacts who were able to pull strings, or call in favours, in order to achieve the very best for their highly rated offspring.

It goes without saying that I was unsuccessful in achieving the position I had been seeking; however, I was offered a job as a boy-labourer out in the yard, which was an all-weather unclean outdoor position, befitting my social class and my religion.

I thanked them very much for their kind consideration of my merits and achievements, but on this occasion, I would decline their kind offer in deference to any Academy pupil who was more deserving than myself (said tongue-in-cheek).

My next interview was with the apprentice supervisor of Kincaid's, whose office was very small and basic in appearance.

Having reviewed my qualifications and digested my answers to any further queries he had regarding my application, I was on my way out without being successful, when he had one final question for me.

'By the way, where does your father work?'

I replied with, 'He has worked here for about thirty years.'

His response was immediate. 'Come back and sit down. Can you start on Monday?'

He may have been expecting me to be wearing a broad smile upon my face as I resumed my seat, but my initial thought was to smack him in the mouth because all my educational hard work and qualifications meant nothing to him. My job offer was only available because of my father's length of service.

That father who had never spoken to me once in all my life, and to whom I would now owe a debt of gratitude.

The man of the house, the person who was charged with overseeing the care of each member of his family, the man who never once intervened on my behalf to protect me from the beatings, bullying, and sexual abuse perpetrated against me within his household!

My thinking at that point was that he had never done anything to support me previously, and, given the chance, he would not willingly support me now.

For that reason, I chose to defy my own will to reject that job offer, and to make use of the nepotism system which existed within that company.

Until my dying day, I would never acknowledge my use of a system which would make my father feel that I owed him something.

During the interview I had expressed an interest in becoming a draughtsman, and following my acceptance of employment, the apprentice manager advised me that I would need to follow the normal apprenticeship route within the company.

He added that during each year an apprentice is usually selected to be transferred to the drawing office.

Having been assigned through a few different sections within the firm, it became clear that my training was destined to ensure that, at the end of my apprenticeship, my title as a journeyman would be "marine engineering fitter".

Whilst I was undergoing training within the finishing shop I was assigned to work under Bill, whose friend on the next bench was Ben. Strange but true.

They were both in their early sixties, and it became obvious to me that some folk never grow up. My work ethic was always to work hard, and to never become a slacker by using idle gossip just to waste time.

Whilst I was working on my project, they would often talk loudly together, in close proximity to me, in order that I would have no doubt concerning the nature of their conversation, which was in reference to me.

Ben, in one conversation, said, 'Do you think he knows what to do?'

Bill responded with, 'Oh, I'm sure he does.'

'What makes you so sure?' queried Ben.

'Well,' replied Bill, 'he must know by now that it's for more than just peeing with!'

Of course, I just continued working away as if they weren't even there. Those two were, so far, the oldest playground kids I'd ever come across, and I didn't expect to find them in a place of work.

It would be during my next move within my apprentice-ship merry-go-round that I was approached on-site by the apprentice supervisor.

He started the conversation by telling me that this year, two apprentices would be moved into the drawing office.

He mentioned Harry, stating that he had already passed a certain qualification, and he would automatically be the first choice.

I told him that, obviously, that was an appropriate choice to make.

The next positional choice was between me and Fred, he added.

He continued by saying that it was a difficult decision to make between us, but that he thought Fred was marginally ahead of me, therefore he would get the second place for transfer into the drawing office.

I told him that I was really happy for Fred, that he was a nice guy, and that I was not annoyed at his progress at my expense.

Fred's current placement was within the millwrights' department, which was on an elevated level, overlooking the point where the apprentice supervisor and I were having our conversation.

He didn't know that he was the next on the supervisor's list for an on-site visit. Following on from their talk, Fred made his way down to speak to me.

He said he had noticed the conversation taking place between the apprentice supervisor and me and asked me what our talk was about.

I told Fred everything that he told me, following which I held out my hand to offer him my congratulations.

Instead of holding his hand out to me, he held his hand up, with raised index finger, in front of him in a "no-no" motion.

Fred agreed with everything relating to the information I had passed on, but there was an additional sentence that the supervisor had added.

In ending the dialogue with Fred, having told him he was chosen for the drawing office, the supervisor had added, 'Oh! Wait a minute, you're over the qualifying age for transfer. I'm sorry!'

I told Fred that that was a disgusting way to be treated by the apprentice supervisor, and if that was right, he should have prepared himself properly before having that talk with him.

Fred then questioned why the supervisor hadn't come back to speak to me again, which was a valid question, and I told him I'd wait to see what happened next.

About a week later I heard that a younger apprentice had been transferred into the drawing office.

As soon as I heard that news, I immediately went to see the apprentice supervisor. Without knocking, I barged into his office, and I was unconcerned about any punishment which might befall me as a result.

There was a look of shock and fear on his face, as he had no idea what was happening, and he pushed his chair backwards away from his desk and the office door, then rose to his feet.

'What kind of game are you playing?' I said to him in a raised voice.

'What's going on? Why are you here? What do you want?' he asked in a fearful voice.

'Did you honestly think your lies wouldn't be found out?' I queried angrily.

His response was just as I expected, as he tried to deny all knowledge of what I was talking about.

I continued with, 'Let me remind you of the conversation that transpired last week when you came to see me; the one where you mentioned that Harry, because of his educational achievements, would be the first of two apprentices being moved into the drawing office!' I stated firmly and confidently as I focused firmly upon his eyes.

'Following on from which, you then told me you had made comparisons between Fred and me and had decided that Fred would be the other apprentice who would be moving into the drawing office. Do you now understand why I'm here?'

Looking less fearful now, he seemed to be more confident that he would be capable of getting onto the front foot again, as he tried to explain that I hadn't qualified for transfer, a fact of which he had previously advised me.

I could see that he felt more in control now, as he sat down again and brought his chair back closer to his desk.

Remaining standing, in order to keep towering over him, I folded my arms to convey the impression to him that I did not fear him.

I told him he was quite correct in everything he had just uttered, but I also advised him, in no uncertain terms, that he was deliberately withholding relevant information, which was damaging to his own credibility, and also that of the company.

Furthermore, I told him he was guilty of lies and deceit, failure of duty of care in respect of his obligations to the company's apprentices, and misuse of powers in order to benefit his preferred choice of potential candidate for advancement within the company.

'I've no idea what you're talking about, and you must leave my office now!' he said.

'I will certainly leave your office,' I said, 'but only after I've finished saying my piece.'

'Having told me that Harry had gained entry to the drawing office on the basis of his educational merits, and that Fred had gained entry because he was marginally better than me, you were deluding yourself if you thought that Fred would not let me know that you told him that he actually did not qualify for entry.'

'On that basis, you should have come back to me, but you didn't. Instead, you chose a younger, less experienced, less well-educated apprentice and moved him into the drawing office. How do you justify that decision?'

It came as no surprise to me that such a stupid answer could come out of the mouth of such a stupid person.

'He has better prospects,' he uttered.

'Damn right he has, with you holding his hand!' I shouted. 'Why can't you just be honest for once in your life? Your choice was based entirely on the fact that Fred and I were both of the Catholic faith, and you would always look after your own kind!'

With my finger pointing into his face during my outburst, I waited there for his reaction, which never came. I then slammed the office door shut as I left.

There were two things I was sure of as I returned to my workspace. Firstly, he had no answers to my accusations, and therefore he was guilty as charged. Secondly, I knew he would take no action against me for my outburst. He knew fine well that I would have brought in the Union to fight my case, and the whole saga would have highlighted his misdeeds throughout the whole company, and his reputation would have been destroyed.

Including my apprenticeship period, I worked for a total of twenty-four years within that company.

Six years after my apprenticeship, which was ten years after joining the firm, my naïvety was once again brought to the forefront of my mind.

My work focus was based on doing the best job possible, and I was unaware of an unrealised truth uttered by me during my apprenticeship period.

Unbeknown to me, the firm had its very own Masonic lodge, referred to as KEMA, which would be of benefit to their lodge members and offspring, as well as any other extended family members, throughout their journey within the company.

My reference regarding the incident of Fred and myself having been deprived of access to the drawing office, several years earlier, was indeed "a true word" although it was never spoken in jest, but out of naïvety on my part.

Throughout my life, my characteristic was to take people at face value. Again, naïvely, I didn't realise the duplicity which people were capable of hiding behind, as opposed to being open and honest, in order to gain advantage over others whilst pretending to be a friend.

In actual fact, as I worked on the shop floor throughout my time in Kincaid's, I had dealings with a variety of folk, and there was never a time when I felt I had been mistreated by anyone.

I think, on the management side, it was just people abusing their power to make personal choices in favour of those who knew how to have the proper handshake at the point of decision making.

Over a period of some years many things transpired which changed the dynamics of the pathway of my life, which will be mentioned at this point.

All my siblings had married and moved out into their own homes and had started their own families. I had no contact from that point onwards with any of them.

I still resided at the same address with my parents, with whom I continued to have little or no contact. My father and I were still estranged from each other, as had always been the case, which was a situation entirely instigated by him from the moment of my birth.

I no longer had any dealings with the Scouts, nor any real connection with the church. Having been inveigled into the church choir at some point, it was something which, in my view, was not properly formed and was just a collection of people who turned up when they felt like it, and so I ceased attending that also.

The lady who was responsible for dressing the altar with flowers for every important religious occasion, along with her son, Tony, was very friendly with my mother.

Inevitably, since he was also part of the choir, Tony became friendly with me and there were times when we played chess in their home as his mother made food for us.

From my point of view there was no strong bond between us and I thought he was actually more friendly with my mother, which made them both untrustworthy in my opinion.

Most nights my mother went out to bingo as there was no conversation between us anyway, and she had company there.

Some nights Tony would arrive where I was living whilst my mother was out. I'm pretty sure they had talked with each other at some point, unbeknown to me, where he was able to find out from her that she thought I was gay.

Since she was aware of all of the sexual activity I had been forced to be part of, at the hands of her older sons, she was making that assumption.

He would have already confessed to her that, as he was gay, he could maybe help me come to terms with it.

Part of the arrangement would have been that he would tell her everything he could about me, knowing she would find out nothing directly from me.

I know that there were times when they had private conversations in her kitchen and conspired with each other behind my back.

Tony was a fair bit older than me, and we did have some discussions. He was very brash and brazen and could have easily been a member of the Gestapo, due to his fierce looks and aggressive attitude.

He visited me one night and brought a young guy with him called John. They had apparently met whilst he was taking delivery of the church flowers to his home whilst his mother was out one Saturday afternoon.

I believe they met up with each other a few times even though there was a substantial age gap between them.

During one of those visits, John told Tony about his pal, George, and how he was hoping to meet someone he might like.

They had been pals throughout their school years, as well as during their weekend part-time jobs working for the same employer.

They were aware that they were both gay, but there was nothing more between them than just being best pals, who would freely talk about anyone to whom they might be attracted.

George had made it known to John that he hoped to meet someone older quite soon, with a view to spending some time with them to see if there was any spark.

John said he knew that Tony had a friend and maybe he could arrange a meeting with him.

Tony agreed that John and George could accompany him next time he visited me.

By now my own life consisted of work, eat, and sleep, with being just home alone most nights watching television. There was no access to computers or such like, and no friends or acquaintances to spend time with.

This was not something which bothered me, as I was used to being in my own company for most of my young life, due to the behaviour of the "family/gang" who had used and abused me from a very early age, excluding the couple of years I spent in Billy's company after school, which were amazing.

heaven;

One night there was an unexpected knock on the door, and it was Tony, his friend John, and someone else whom I didn't know, but who John introduced to me as his pal George.

We sat and blethered, and after a while, I was advised there was a specific reason for their visit, which they would now divulge.

Of the four of us in that room, I was the only one who was not aware that I was on a blind date. It was then that John explained matters to me.

George sat very quietly during the early conversation, apparently watching me and listening to me, which was something I didn't realise was happening.

There must have been some sort of signal between them which indicated that George had formed a positive opinion of me.

I'm guessing there was a back-up plan of non-disclosure regarding the reason for their visit, in the event of a negative opinion of me from George.

It was then suggested that George and I should get to know each other a bit better.

Although I was shocked and stunned by the course of events, I stood up and held out my hand towards George, whereby he stood up and took hold of mine. We walked up the hallway together to my room and closed the door.

The situation between us was different to that between Billy and me, because there was no need for me to protect George in the same way as I did with Billy, but I still felt the need to be cautious with my behaviour.

I asked him if it was OK to hug him, and he moved closer into my chest where we put our arms around each other, and our cheeks made contact.

Soon after that, I asked if it was OK to kiss him. He moved his lips onto mine, and we gently kissed.

I felt it was important to get his consent, and make sure he agreed with our limited physical contact. Our age difference could prove problematic for me otherwise.

We then sat on the edge of the bed and began to talk, in order to find out more about each other. During the information exchanges, some more hugging and gentle kissing transpired, as we continued to become more familiar with each other.

Enough time had been spent becoming acquainted for now, as it was getting closer to the time for my mother's return home, so we hugged and kissed one last time, then we joined the other two, and they all left, leaving me unexpectedly happy.

I had made no further arrangements to meet him again as there were some things I really needed to think about.

There was no doubt he was attractive, as well as being of a similar shy nature to mine. Two issues though, required me to seriously consider the way ahead.

The first concern centred around whether, having lived a solo life for several years, did I need, or was I ready for, a relationship with any other person at all.

Secondly, and with specific regard to George, was the issue of the age gap between us. Certainly, I was drawn to him when we first met, which was another factor, but there were nine years between us. I was twenty-five and he was only sixteen.

One other thing I noticed when we were getting acquainted with each other was that he tended to follow my lead. Whatever movement I made, he copied. I knew that I would not lead him astray, nor mistreat or abuse him, but if he was to be with anyone else, who knew how he might be treated or what might happen to him. This was another consideration for me.

I still felt the need to be his protector.

I had no direct way of making contact with him, and almost a week had transpired since our first meeting.

I thought it would only be right and proper to arrange to meet him personally, so arranged through Tony to get a message to him that I could pick him up and take him for a drive in the car.

Word came back of when and where to pick him up.

Although he seemed quiet and shy, like me, he was quite straightforward in his first comment. 'When I didn't hear from you, I thought you didn't want me!'

That wasn't said in a hurtful or aggressive way. He was just eager to know in which direction his future might be heading.

We bought some ice cream from the Esplanade Café in Greenock and returned to the car to talk privately.

I explained to him the reasons for not contacting him before now, and told him of my concerns. He seemed to be concentrating on my face as he was still not sure what I was going to be saying.

I told him I was perfectly willing to have him as my boyfriend if that was what he wished for.

His eyes lit up and a broad smile spread over his face as he sought clarification with, 'Really! You're not kidding me?'

I reached for his hand and held it tightly as I told him, 'Seriously, George, I'm looking forward to being with you.'

The car started to vibrate as if he was jumping for joy, even though he was still strapped into the seat. We exchanged contact details as we set about linking our lives together.

As expected, I shared no information with my mother, and I'm sure she wondered why I was hardly ever at home from then on.

As the days, weeks, and months passed, we became inseparable and closer together in our love. George's mother was also curious about where her son was going and with whom.

She could see from her window that he took a shortcut through the nearby school grounds before getting into a car. She mentioned it so much within George's hearing that we changed the pick-up point for our meetings.

George and his mother were really close to each other, as opposed to his three older brothers, who were more aligned with their father.

The similarities between George's family and mine were amazing. His family consisted of mother, father, and four siblings, which were three older brothers and George. Like me, George was the baby of his family.

Coming up in the near future was his parents' silver

wedding anniversary, which would be held at their home, and George decided to invite me to attend. They were very popular with their neighbours, so their house was going to be packed with people on that night.

This was George's way of introducing me to the whole family and friends.

Naturally, at the event I knew no-one except George so I kind of felt out of place. I acquired a chair in the corner of the room whilst George was rather busy looking after the needs of the neighbours, although he hadn't abandoned me.

As well as looking after me, he had arranged for others to bring me goodies as a way of having them introduce themselves to me and chat a bit. I did feel that I was being made welcome and did not feel out of place.

They understood I was George's guest, was made welcome, and invited back often enough to feel almost part of the family already.

In later days, there were many times when his father made lunch for me whilst George had gone back to work, having already had his lunch. We worked for different companies, and our lunch breaks were never the same.

During the times having lunch in George's dad's company, no questions were ever asked about our relationship, and there was no awkwardness between us.

The relationship between George and me was getting stronger, and we treated each other as equals, discussing all plans together, with neither of us trying to force the other to be somewhere, or do something we weren't happy with.

Looking at George's face, it was really obvious that he was in love, and he was forever asking me if he could do anything for me, buy something for me, or get me something to eat.

Although he was much younger than I, he was most definitely not out to live off me; he would always be willing to put his hand in his pocket. When we were in clothes shops, he was always telling me to pick something out and he would pay for it.

The joy he brought into my life was unbelievable, and the wonderful smile on his face brought me so much happiness every day. His happiness was my highest priority.

There could never be a time when I would be angry with him, for he had such a wonderful personality.

Truth be told, in comparison, I was much more mundane, probably due to the treatment received throughout my childhood. I could never understand why he was so attracted to me.

We set about finding a place where we could effectively live together, and luckily we managed to acquire some student accommodation which served as our first home, where we could properly be together as a couple in every sense of the word.

Soon it would be time to tell my mother that I would be moving out, but there would be "no meat on the bones" with this notification, such as where I'd be moving, or with whom I'd be living.

Within a couple of days, I was gone from that God-forsaken hellhole.

Unlike me, George would still be in contact with both of his parents on a daily basis.

We were 100% in support of each other and watched each other's back for anyone who was out to show dissent towards either of us. This was not by arrangement, just part of our love for each other.

We would defend each other and not cover up whatever might have been said, even if it was said by someone we regarded as a friend.

Although George was aware of my treatment at the hands of my family, he still had a desire to meet my mother at some point, which was not something I was keen on.

I would not deny his wish though, and we arrived there one afternoon about a week later. I just introduced him as, 'This is George,' without any other information.

She offered to make something to eat, but in my view, that was to hide in the kitchen for a while.

George and I had never talked about his reason for wanting to meet her, but in her company he showed her his charming side and wonderful smile, and was also able to carry the conversation quite naturally.

After we had left her house, we spoke about what was on his mind.

In the first instance, he was wondering if she regretted having lost contact with me; might she offer an apology for her previous behaviour, or maybe seek to make amends?

In seeing me again, would she recognise this visit as being an opportunity in which to try to reconnect with me?

Secondly, she would see that her youngest son was in the company of someone who was very mannerly, pleasant, and more than happy to be by his side.

If the information she had previously received about her son being gay was believed by her and was a situation of which she did not approve, she could not deny that our happiness in being together was obvious whilst sitting there on her settee.

From my perspective, though, the time for her to show her disapproval of my being gay would have been at the point when I told her about her two paedophile eldest sons, and their individual sexual abuse of me, her ten-year-old innocent and youngest son, all those years ago.

There is no accusation that they made me gay, though, as it's well established that people are born gay, and don't have a choice in the matter.

It's entirely possible, though, that parents or siblings can see that their family member is gay from a very early age, whilst the child doesn't know about it until they are older, although sometimes even before puberty arrives.

Such cruelty should never have been inflicted on any young kid, for so many years, by his entire family, with no remorse ever having been felt, or shown, towards their innocent youngest son and sibling, who deserved to know and feel only their utmost love and care.

There is also the possibility that a gay child could be used, abused, or bullied for being gay by family members, even before the child knows the reason for such torment happening within the "loving" family home.

It was also my view that there was nothing different about my leaving her household now, than it would have been if I had left because I was in a "normal" marriage situation, to set up home elsewhere with whomsoever I was in love with.

George and I were most definitely a couple in love who would share our lives together then, and for eternity.

Meeting him was the most wonderful day of my life, and he vowed to cherish me, and provide me with all the love and happiness of which I had been deprived for my entire childhood.

We followed our own routine each night during the week as we settled into bed. George would be first into bed whilst I would turn off any unnecessary electrics and ensure doors and windows were securely locked. Quite by chance, neither of us felt comfortable in pyjamas, and each wore only a T-shirt and nothing else.

We would lie in the dark facing each other initially, as we talked about our plans for the next morning and where we would be going. We believed in being out quite early each day and would agree to head to Clydebank, Linwood, Braehead, or the like.

Prior to settling down, we would give each other a peck on the cheek, and George would decide which one of us would lovingly cuddle into the other.

Not every night, but quite often, we would wake up during the night, which would often be around 3am.

There was never any pre-planning, but that point would be when we were most amorous with each other, after which we would again cuddle together and go back to sleep.

Without any discussion or planning, it just seemed to be the case that I became an adopted member of George's family, no questions asked.

Perhaps his parents recognised how happy and confident their son had become, as a result of my influence over the direction of George's life, and that brought them contentment, pride, and joy.

At the earliest point possible, I started teaching George how to drive and he seemed to adapt to it quite well. When I thought he was proficient enough, I applied for his driving test.

Just before his test was due, though, I arranged for a driving instructor to assess his driving over a prolonged lesson on the same day as his test.

On completion of that assessment, the instructor stated that George was not ready to sit a test and would need a lot more lessons before he was ready.

As George started his test on Greenock's Esplanade, I have to confess I spent most of the time sitting in the nearby Esplanade toilet block, worrying about how he was managing.

When the test was over and the car returned to the driving examiner's office, George gave me the test result paperwork, which showed he had passed. I was so pleased and proud of his first-time pass. *Shows how much the instructor knows*, I thought to myself. Due process meant his full licence would now need to be applied for, and for him to be added onto my insurance certificate.

An unexpected benefit of being in our student accommodation was meeting several other nearby gay couples with whom we could meet up and spend some time.

As well as being at a few parties in their abodes, we could meet up in the popular gay pubs.

To our surprise, in our first visit to the most popular establishment, there was someone we recognised from our home town.

We really didn't expect to see, wearing civilian clothes, and having a great time in the company of a much younger guy, one of the priests from our local church. We deliberately moved ourselves to an area of the bar where he couldn't see us, in order not to cause him any embarrassment or anxiety, in the event that he realised he had been spotted by us, and that we might spill the beans when back in the parish.

I was not at all surprised to find a priest there, due to previous observations within our own parish.

Going back to the period of time I had spent in Billy's company, when he was an altar server, and I would wait outside for him after Mass, there was a fair amount of time before he came out.

The priest in charge of the altar boys, Fr Watson, kept him in his company much longer than was necessary. Also, he always arranged that Billy was the only one who served on the altar with him.

I believed he used that time to be closer to him and spend more time with him because he was attracted to him; although I had no evidence to support my thoughts.

Perhaps I was just concerned for Billy's safety. I would always protect him from coming to any harm from me, so I wouldn't allow anyone else to take advantage of him.

Billy and I cycled to Loch Lomond, to spend a week camping on its shores one summer, and I heard the put-putting of a motor scooter engine coming to a stop nearby on one of those days.

Fr Watson had arrived unexpectedly and spent some time lying beside Billy inside the tent, although the tent door was wide open.

I had no option other than to remain outside the two-man tent as, quite clearly, he was not there to talk to me during his visit; but then again, I had been previously aware of his jealousy of my friendship with Billy.

When there were functions within the church hall, I would always sit at the same table as Billy's parents and would always sit next to Billy.

Fr Watson would be sitting on the apron of the stage, close by, where he could watch Billy and me enjoying ourselves in each other's company. The word "enjoying" is probably not a very apt description of his thinking about our friendship.

There were times when it was necessary for me to have to speak to Fr Watson during these functions, and he was always unpleasant to me, if no-one else was close enough to hear his attitude.

As alluded to earlier, priests in gay bars were not a surprise to me.

By now we had agreed to move away from our student abode, as we wanted to move into our own place; also, although we had met and made friends with several other couples, there were issues which we disliked.

Several of the couples were forever arguing or bickering, even in company, and we failed to understand their kind of love; it was not the kind of love we felt for each other.

We loved and adored each other to such an extent that fighting or arguing was just unthinkable.

We jointly bought a three-bed semi in Bearsden around the same time that George accepted a job in Dykebar hospital. This was in the locked ward and was on the night shift.

I was amazed that George was confident enough and capable of travelling those roads at night on his own, and also working in the locked ward took courage, yet he performed his duties with distinction.

So much so that, after a while, he was approached by the powers that be, to be told they wanted to train him properly in the field of psychiatric nursing.

Whilst it was an honour to be chosen, George declined the offer.

He gave no reason for not accepting, but they continued to try to subtly persuade him.

On arrival each night at work, there would be an envelope waiting for him, which contained work-related literature relative to the post on offer.

What they succeeded in doing though, was forcing him to resign his post.

George knew exactly his own limitations and was aware he would never be able to fulfil the requirements of the job.

He explained to me his reasons, which were perfectly understandable.

A nurse on any ward would have a lot of paperwork per patient to do daily. Within that paperwork would be notes relating to their medication.

Reflecting on himself, he had some prescribed medicines to be taken daily. He knew how complicated the names of them were, both to try to speak, or to spell.

There was no way he would be willing to risk harm to any patient, however slim that risk might be, as a result of his own limitations in trying to master a system which, in his own view, was needlessly Latinised or elitist in nature.

He obtained employment at Inverclyde Royal Hospital in the transport section, where his duties were various.

Every hospital in the surrounding area, including those which required ferry travel to reach, needed clean laundry delivered and dirty laundry uplifted. George was one of the team of drivers who carried out those duties weekly.

There were also patients whose medical supplies had to be delivered to their homes as these were bulk item deliveries, which were also part of George's remit.

Additionally, George had potentially dangerous duties to be carried out two evenings per week.

He was responsible for driving the needle-exchange van into the two local drugs hotspots. There was a single nurse on board who would check the addicts' puncture wounds, clean and dress as necessary, and exchange their old needles for new ones.

Overall, George was responsible for the nurse's safety and security throughout her two-hour stay on these sites, but that wasn't easy, as he was not allowed access to the rear of the van whilst a patient was on board, as their privacy was paramount.

He was allowed to spend time with the nurse if there were no clients on board the van but had to return to his cabin if a patient arrived. George had a wonderful sense of humour, and he kept the nurse thoroughly amused during those needle-exchange shifts, especially on the dark winter evenings.

We sold our Bearsden home shortly after George's dad passed away. George, as previously mentioned, loved his mother very much, so we bought a local three-bed home, and his mother lived with us thereafter.

George enjoyed attending some of the local social clubs at the weekend and made many friends there. He enjoyed dancing to all of the various bands, and was naturally adept at all forms of dancing. He never required dancing lessons; the music just set him off flawlessly. He especially had everyone's attention when he was gyrating during rock-n-roll or jive numbers.

When the night was coming to a close, many folks approached him to say how much they appreciated the amount of pleasure he had brought to their night, and were looking forward to seeing him next weekend.

His dancing in the clubs had been part of his life from early on during our time together, as there was no requirement to work any weekends. I was certainly not gifted like he was, but I was delighted he received so much praise and appreciation.

I was happy for him; I could never be jealous of him.

There was one particular Saturday night when it was his birthday; his twenty-second, I think.

It had been a hot summer's day; the club was very busy and inside the hall it was very clammy.

The band that night was particularly good, and George was dancing almost constantly. Some of his friends of a similar age were aware of the need to ensure he remained on the dance floor.

They knew it was time for their birthday present to him to arrive. Miss Busty, the strip-o-gram, bounced in the door and captured him in front of the stage.

There was a lot of noise in the hall from all the patrons, at the sight of Miss Busty, although she was more like Miss Bulky.

The first part of her show was to read out a poem to George, although George, with all his dancing, the heat, and some drink, was soaking wet with sweat.

She tried to put her arm around him, and then realised how wet he was. As she tried to draw away from him, he pulled her into him, making her thoroughly soaking wet.

The punters were ecstatic with cheers, laughter, and catcalls, as she struggled to be heard.

The next part of her act was for George to remove her garter from her thigh with his teeth.

Everything about her performance had George in stitches, so much so that he couldn't complete the task for laughing. He gave the impression of completing it by grabbing it with his hand as he stood up whilst waving it in the air.

The crowd went wild, and they all suddenly started to chant, 'Get them aff. Get them aff.'

George was having so much fun that maybe he didn't realise their chanting was for Miss Busty.

Next minute his trousers were round his ankles, his hands were behind his head, and his hips were in full pelvic thrust mode, as his trademark smile covered the whole width of his face.

The noise from the audience could have taken the roof off the joint.

This was my George at his very best. I was so very pleased for him, and so proud of him; he was having so much fun and providing so much entertainment to so many people.

Most of the crowd dispersed as soon as the night was over, but a party of six ladies remained seated near the back of the hall. One of them, it seemed, actually knew George, and called on him.

They told him how much they had enjoyed their night, but missed his strip show because everyone was standing up and blocking their view.

In order to satisfy his fans, he obliged with a repeat performance.

It seemed to me though, that George could be at risk as they were squealing in pleasure, stretching out their arms and hands towards him whilst also trying to touch him. I then got in between them, and suggested to George that he should move away, and get ready to leave to a place of safety.

That was probably the most memorable birthday party ever within that social club, which now no longer exists.

There was a day when George's mother asked him to take her to buy a new dress for a friend's daughter's wedding. She was very pleased with her new purchase but when crossing the road back to George's car, she collapsed onto the road and became unconscious.

An ambulance took her to hospital whilst he waited and called me because he was too worried and upset to drive.

I secured his car, which we would collect later, and tried to comfort him in my car prior to taking him to the Glasgow hospital which the ambulance crew had said would be their destination.

We waited at the hospital for an update on her condition, but the staff advised they wouldn't know for several hours. They said she was currently on a life-support machine whilst they assessed her condition and awaited the results of tests.

Their suggestion was for us to go home, and they would give an update by phone call around 10pm.

As George was clearly really upset, I agreed this would be the best plan as I could hold him in my arms and try to comfort him as best as I could in the meantime.

When the hospital called, George was dreading whatever news he was about to receive. I stood cuddled into his back with my arms around his waist; he held the phone in his right hand whilst his left hand tightly grasped both of my hands which supported his waist.

'We have to advise you that your mother has had a brain haemorrhage. We are very sorry and are doing all we can. We also must explain to you that some time tomorrow, we might need to seek your permission to disconnect her from the life-support machine.'

George knew that I could hear the conversation. At that point, he pushed the phone into my hand, knowing that I would take control from that point onwards, as he was too upset.

I could feel George's legs buckling beneath him, as I told the spokesman, 'I understand, thanks.'

George really did understand there was no hope of any recovery for his beloved mother but was also adamant he would never be able to authorise switching off the machine.

We lay side by side on top of the bed as I gently caressed the temples of his forehead, whilst wiping his tears as they slowly ran down his cheeks.

We changed positions several times as I hugged and caressed him, knowing fine well that it was his mother's love which mattered most to him right now, and also knowing that his love for me was no less diminished.

Each of us had our own place in his beautiful and loving heart, sharing equally of his love for the mother who gave birth to him and raised him, and of the partner who brought him personal love, joy, pleasure, and protection.

We lay arm-in-arm for hours as George recalled many tales and memories, through his tears, of his mother's trials and tribulations, until we finally fell asleep, after which we were awakened by the sound of the phone ringing around 7am.

We stood up, and once again we adopted the same pose as for the previous phone call from the hospital. This phone call opened with apologies that George's mother had just passed away and an invitation to collect the death certificate and personal belongings.

Even though we were aware that this outcome was expected, George was at least relieved he did not have to be the one to authorise the life-support machine to be shut down. That would have been a burden too much for him to bear, not only at that moment of time, but forever more within his conscience.

He knew that people would now need to be told the news, we both did, but my duty was to comfort him first of all.

I returned him gently back to bed as I cuddled warmly into his back; my arms were lightly folded around his waist with one hand ensuring that a sufficient quantity of tissues was close by. My cheek was able to rest gently upon his, in order that he knew how much sympathy, support, and love I had to offer him.

The day of his mother's funeral would be a time when I would need to keep a discreetly close eye on him, especially during the ceremony.

As I was uncertain how he would be able to cope, I would be very close behind him because he would have the number one cord, at the head of the coffin, as she was lowered into the grave.

I trusted absolutely that his love for her would give him the strength, physically and mentally, to complete the task, but I remained close to him in order to be prepared to love, support, and protect him through any sign of weakness or distress.

Around three or four months had passed since the funeral when the enormity of his loss caused George to suffer severe depression, which also seemed to affect a variety of nerves, tendons, and some joints.

His G.P. had prescribed various medications which were each part of various regimes which must be tried and tested prior to him being referred to a specialist hospital consultant.

He was now regularly attending his consultant where his medications were often reviewed.

His consultant was now part of a team of consultants who would regularly meet and discuss each other's patients, and collectively agree each patient's ongoing course of treatment.

George's meds were now completely revised to a system whereby he had now to inject a fixed dose of a liquid into his thigh.

Gradually he would increase the dosage from one jab in one thigh, to alternative thighs, and then to each thigh.

It might be the case that all those patients could be on the same medications in order to monitor the effects or responses from one patient to another. Without their knowledge, this group of patients might be taking part in a trial.

They also were supplied with sharps boxes along with each new set of needle injection drugs.

George seemed to manage the administration of this prescription relatively easily.

During all the years that George and I were together, our relationship had always been something which was extra special.

It wasn't just love; it was more than that, it was a joint need and a joint trust: It was a commitment, it was way beyond that. We had to always support one another, be close to each other, and be each other's strength.

To feel that someone truly loves you, in every kiss you share, in every warm and lasting hug in their arms, in every intimate, thrilling, and personal touch; that was our love so far.

Although the loss of his mother caused George to suffer from depression, over a period of time we developed a method to aid him to cope slightly better, and to partly return to enjoying life again.

We returned to being out and about early each morning again, meeting up with his closest friends, and returning to dancing to the familiar music of his favourite entertainers during his free time over the weekends.

We also added something new to his agenda by arranging foreign holidays a couple of times each year. I suppose it might be regarded as a bit cheesy to suggest these gave him "blue Spanish eyes".

None of this could be regarded as a cure though, as there were still some issues to deal with, usually at home, when there was just the two of us.

I think when he was relaxing in his own thoughts, there was no way for me to know what was on his mind.

I was torn between giving him peace and quiet, or seeming to quiz or harass him, which might distress him, which I never wanted to do.

A bit of love and care came into my head as well, but I was thinking I might just be seen as taking advantage of him.

Overall, I think his friends had assessed that his public persona was generally returning closer to normality.

Our life and our love together were important factors, especially during difficult times.

Knowing that a hug and a kiss were only a couple of feet away from you at a moment's notice, was a very comforting and uplifting thought to retain at the forefront of your mind.

As previously mentioned, it was difficult to know what was on his mind, but there was one night, as he was stretched out on the settee, when George made a statement which absolutely floored me.

'Both our families have all gone, and we only have each other now, no-one else. I want to go before you.

You are strong enough to cope without me. If you were to go first, I couldn't live without you. I would kill myself,' he stated.

I tried to show no facial expression upon hearing his words, and calmly replied, 'George, trust me, I will always be by your side. You never have to worry about anything. Please, babe, always put your trust in me. I will never let you down.'

I approached the settee and held out my hand to him as I said, 'Let's dance.'

We put our arms around each other and shuffled around the floor, resting our foreheads together. The shuffling ended when we reached the bed, where we enjoyed the pleasures of each other's bodies before spooning together to settle down for the night.

My hope was that, come morning time, those thoughts would have disappeared from his mind forever more.

I now had a better grasp of what troubled George as a result of his statement. Quite clearly, he relied on feeling that he was fully supported by someone he trusted, someone who would always protect him. Having lost his entire family, he had only me now, and worried about being left alone if he lost me too.

Next morning George seemed to be in a brighter mood as we prepared to set off on one of our typical days out.

He always enjoyed breakfast upstairs in McGonigal's boat-shaped restaurant in Clydebank, followed by visiting some of his favourite stores which stocked ornamental items, which were very much to his liking, as, despite his ongoing bouts of depression, he continued to take pride in our home: our love nest.

There was one morning though, when he felt

slightly breathless, and made an appointment to visit the doctor.

Certain things about such visits were always predictable, in that it would be the practice nurse we would see, and we both would go into the consulting room. George needed support in these situations and it was never questioned that I was always there with him.

Generally, he would ask me to explain things outside of the consultation in order to understand what she meant.

George told the nurse about feeling slightly breathless.

Regardless of the reason why George had requested the appointment, the nurse would always do a full check-up, probably because of his meds, including him injecting his own thighs.

At the point where she was checking his blood pressure and oxygen levels on a finger monitor, she seemed unsure of the results and left the room. She returned with a doctor and they both used different finger monitors on different hands.

The outcome was that George was told he must go immediately to Inverclyde Royal Hospital. I spoke on George's behalf by stating, 'He wasn't expecting that.'

The doctor said she would give him a letter for IRH explaining the reason for him being sent there.

As I drove George to the hospital, I have to say that he didn't seem concerned about what was occurring, or what might happen.

He was quickly allocated a bed in a ward, and the plan was to connect him to an oxygen supply to increase his oxygen level over a period of time, and to monitor its effect.

George had never been in hospital before but seemed to be quite calm and would chat on the phone to friends, as well as with those who would visit him.

After a while he was told by clinicians that they had to increase the oxygen levels to a greater level as insufficient progress was being made.

Next day they moved him into intensive care as that ward facilitated a greater level of oxygen than any other ward in the hospital.

I and other visitors were with him during the afternoon visiting period that same day when a nurse approached me with a request to go with her to see George's consultant. She was the one who was responsible for prescribing the meds which he was injecting into his thighs.

He still had visitors with him as I left with the nurse and was cheery enough as I looked back at him.

The consultant, I and the nurse sat in an unused ward, and she began to talk about George's circumstances.

I have to confess that I couldn't understand a word of what she was saying as it seemed too technical. I felt, though, that this was an apology, which ended by her saying that George would be attached to a life-support machine and moved to the intensive care ward in Royal Alexandra Hospital in Paisley.

When I returned to George, he no longer had visitors even though visiting period hadn't yet ended.

I told him what his consultant said about a life-support machine and Paisley hospital.

He told me a doctor had asked his visitors to leave, after which the doctor told him about the life-support machine and movement to Paisley.

On hearing what George said, I was absolutely livid

that he had had no-one to support him when he was given such information.

The whole reason for my always being with him was to support and protect him, to be able to explain to him things that he didn't, or couldn't, understand, and to remind him that I was always right there beside him.

Although I was livid, I remained facially calm, so that he wouldn't worry about my anger. He would be worried enough. He now looked more worried and asked me a serious question, 'Am I going to die?'

Considering that I genuinely thought he was reasonably healthy, my response was kind of flippant as I replied, 'George, don't be silly!'

Just then the porters came for him. Next time I would see him would be the following day in Paisley.

As I sat at home thinking about him, I suddenly realised the reason for his question. His mother died whilst on a life-support machine.

I arrived early at the Intensive Care Unit in RAH in Paisley, as I believed relatives' visiting was not as restricted as in other wards due to the patients' vulnerability.

Security was monitored via intercom by identifying who you were, and the name of the patient you were visiting. You might be requested to wait if the patient was undergoing treatment at that moment.

My time of arrival was 10.15am and I was allowed access without delay. Once through the security door, there was a short corridor, with rooms off, which led to the door of the main ward.

On entering the ward, I was approached by a consultant and was utterly shocked by his first words to me. 'We think his problems are being caused by his medication.'

He guided me to a private room where George lay on a bed elevated to waist height. There were around six clinicians around the bed assessing his condition because he had only arrived late on the previous day.

They had acted very quickly in getting him settled and organised, judging by the various amount of medical equipment, tubes, and such like, which were necessary to maintain and monitor his condition.

My position, as a visitor or relative, was beside his bed just to the left of the entrance to the room. At the other side of the bed was the nurse responsible for his complete care throughout her shift of probably twelve hours.

The foot of the bed was fitted out with a desk area full of all sorts of graphs and data regarding any changes which indicated any improvements, or otherwise, in George's condition, which is where the decision-makers would gather to plot their next course of action.

My first impression was about how very well organised everything was, and how George was never left alone or unattended at any point. His appointed nurse was always checking or adjusting equipment, administering his meds and/or recording all necessary data.

On the downside, in my view, there was no conversation or explanation about what she was doing or why. There was a limited number of times you could ask her, 'What's that you're doing?' or 'What response are you expecting from that?'

Something simple like, 'I'm giving George his meds now, then I need to record his stats,' would have been enough to break the silence whilst being informative.

It went without saying that I would be there every day with George, talking to him and watching whatever treatment he was receiving.

Of course, I wanted to see improvement in his condition as soon as possible, and the consultant wanted me to tell him everything I could about George, in case it might help him to understand what might aid his recovery.

Each day there would be slight changes in his treatment but, to me, it seemed like trial and error.

One afternoon I was asked to a vacant visitors' room as the consultant wanted to give me an update. In the presence of others, he wanted to advise me that, for the whole of next week, he would be on holiday. Another consultant would be in charge of George's care.

There was more important information he needed to make me aware of also.

By the time he returned from holiday, it was unlikely that George would still be here. He added that if he was still with us, he would need round-the-clock care.

Without waiting, my immediate response was that I would always give him my best and utmost care.

'We'll let you rest here for a while,' he said, 'but maybe you want to get yourself a cup of coffee,' he added as he left.

I sat alone for a while thinking about my declaration of how I would give George the best of care, then realised that there was no way George would want to live that kind of life.

My thoughts were then focused on George's words.

I couldn't believe the question he'd asked me whilst in Inverclyde Royal Hospital, when he was told he would be put onto a life-support machine and moved to this Paisley Hospital.

'Am I going to die?' he had asked, with a look of fear in his eyes.

'George, don't be silly!' had been my reply. He in no way appeared to be so ill.

Who would have thought that would be our last ever conversation together?

I continued to visit each and every day without fail, and also continued to talk to him, in the hope that he could hear my voice, even though I didn't know if he could.

The clinicians kept trying different things over each day, including my finding him one morning on a dialysis machine. As always seemed to be the way of things, no explanation was offered as to why.

On driving up to Paisley next day, it occurred to me that this was the Thursday of George's original consultant's holiday week, and he was due to return to work soon.

I wondered what plans or treatment they had in mind for him today.

No obvious changes were in sight as I said, 'Hi, George, how are you today?'

At that moment I was in shock! He turned his face towards me and stared at me. *Wow*, I thought to myself. Did he hear me and recognise my voice?

He returned his head to rest on the pillow, and I waited for a minute or so before speaking again.

'Are you in any pain, George? I'm right here beside you.'

Once again, he turned his face towards me and stared into my eyes. Something was wrong though. He seemed to be blind. There was no blinking of his eyes.

Another change brought about by the clinician was that he was no longer sedated, nor in an induced coma.

That response continued several times after I spoke to him.

He could hear me, recognise my voice, but his eyes could not follow my hand movements. He was now clinically blind and was unable to understand why he could hear me, know where I was standing, but couldn't see me.

There came a point where I was asked to have a coffee break as they needed to turn him.

There were so many things going through my mind as I sat in the hospital café; things I was struggling to comprehend.

When George had said he felt a bit breathless originally, he wasn't struggling to breathe, yet the finger monitors prompted immediate hospital action.

Various levels of oxygen failed to make any improvement in his condition, yet he still was not struggling to breathe.

Once he was attached to the life-support machine, it became impossible for me to gauge if any changes were taking place.

Of the treatments I saw taking place, I had to wonder why there was a need for George's shortness of breath to suddenly require him to be attached to a dialysis machine. What was the connection?

As discovered before the coffee break, why did it appear now, when he was no longer sedated or in an induced coma, that he had lost his sight? What was the connection to his shortness of breath?

The fact that no condition report has been advised or updated to me at any point, raised issues which I would take up with the department leads after the event.

Of course, I had the greatest respect for clinicians of all levels and would never cause any kind of scene within hospital property. I had patience and would follow all protocols.

I returned to the ward but had to wait for access as they were not ready yet.

After a while I was given the OK to enter, and as I was heading towards George's private room, I could see it was empty.

Not knowing what was happening, I stopped in my tracks. His nurse appeared from behind a curtain, to tell me that George had been moved into a bed in the ward and ushered me behind the same curtain from which she had just emerged.

My immediate thought was that she had deliberately *lied* to me, by saying they wanted to turn George.

I was seething at this lie but concealed it as I followed her. Having arrived at George's new bed, I asked her, 'Why?'

'He's no longer infectious now,' was her reply.

The level of seething immediately doubled inside of me, as yet another lie emerged from her mouth.

Very close to two weeks had been spent by me beside George, in his private room, and there had not been one request for me to wear any kind of PPE.

There was clearly a plan being followed, and little or no treatment was destined to be carried out now, on an ongoing basis.

Anger was increasing within me and, despite my respect for hospital premises, I wasn't sure if I could refrain from exploding.

After she disappeared, I realised that she would no longer be in attendance as before. There were fewer medical devices to hand now as well.

I took the decision to leave earlier than usual in order to give me time to calm myself down.

Tomorrow was another day.

Around 4pm that same afternoon I received a phone

call telling me that George had taken a turn for the worse and they weren't sure which way it was going to go.

Whilst driving back up to the hospital, I was thinking again about the events which had transpired earlier on. The first thought was about him no longer being sedated or in an induced coma.

In my mind there was an element of readiness for the next part of their programme.

Stripping him out of the private room and moving him into an ordinary bed in the main ward, with the possibility of less nursing, seemed like phase two of their agenda.

It is entirely possible that my thinking about those issues was only within my imagination, but I tended to stick with my thoughts, to be honest.

I reported to the ward nurse when I arrived, and she told me that I could spend some time with George. When I was ready, I could let her know, and she would turn off the machine!

Why did this seem like the final part of their plan?

What happened to her 'we don't know which way it's going to go' comment on the phone to me less than an hour before?

Lie number three perhaps?

Without mentioning any of these issues for now, which would be raised at a later stage, as previously mentioned, there was an issue I would most definitely raise right then.

The bed in which George currently lay, which would shortly be properly described as his death bed, had been given absolutely no consideration for it to be a suitable place for a peaceful passing.

The patient in the bed in the alcove at the foot of George's bed was screened off entirely from view by a curtain. Access to that patient, be it visitors, or hospital staff, was through the end of the curtain at the foot of that patient's bed.

For that to happen, all those visitors or staff had to pass along the bottom of George's bed which was not screened off.

He had no privacy at any time from anyone seeking access to that alcove bed, not even if intimate procedures were being carried out on George.

I called for the duty nurse and made my complaints.

'I am to say my final farewell to my lover, after forty-six years, as he leaves this world, and all this traffic is happening around us. I would have no idea if our parting was being filmed or recorded on phone cameras, or just even being watched. You must rectify this issue, immediately, and explain why you thought this was acceptable arrangements for loving relatives to endure at such a sad period in their lives!'

Temporary arrangements were put in place, and I was guaranteed there would be nothing happening which would cause any form of interruption.

'Hi George, honey. It's Hugh here, right beside you as I've always been since we first met. I still remember the blind date which I didn't know about, and how we sat on my bed, holding hands, as we got to know each other. Also our first kiss and cuddle, more than one actually, that night.

'After that night though, there were two things I needed to think about, which were potentially a barrier to continuing with our relationship.

'You might have been thinking that, since I was twenty-five, I would have had some experience of being in a loving or sexual relationship before; but I hadn't and wasn't sure if I was ready to indulge in one now.

'The other issue, babe, was your age. At just sixteen, it looked to be too big an age gap. In our first meeting though, we seemed to gel well together, besides which, you were so damned attractive.

'About a week later, we met each other again, and over a tub of ice cream on Greenock's Esplanade, we agreed to be each other's boyfriend.

'An agreement which brings me now to be sitting on this bed, and holding hands with you, forty-six years on from the start.

'Naturally we shared a lifetime of kisses and cuddles, and the joy of being in sexual harmony with each other throughout that lifetime.

'As I sit on this bed now, holding your hands, it will soon be time for us to say goodbye, George, instead of saying hello.

'I remember when your mam was in hospital, and you were told you might be asked for permission to turn off her life-support machine. You loved her so much that you vowed that was something you could never do.

'You didn't have to, though, as she passed away on her own. You shed so many tears and mourned her loss for such a long time. Our love for each other helped you to cope.

'You never forgot her, though.

'As I sit here now, holding your hand, I have already been asked for my permission to turn off the machine which supports your breathing, and reluctantly, I will give my consent soon.

'You and I will be unable to maintain any more physical contact with each other once that has been done.

'The love I have for you means that I should shed a bucket load of tears, and feel so much pain, after losing you, George.

'Instead of that, I will be happy for you. Your happiness means everything to me, and always has.

'That statement you made one night whilst lying on the settee at home, shocked me quite a bit, and was retained within my memory banks. You said, "I want to go first. You can cope without me. I can't live without you. If you go first, I will kill myself."

'George, I said that I would always be beside you, and here I am as promised.

'After the HELL of my childhood, and the PURGATORY of my teenage years, you brought HEAVEN into the rest of my life, and I can't thank you enough for committing yourself to only me for your entire lifespan.

'No words could ever describe the level or depth of my love for you. Although I will have lost all physical contact with you, your spirit cannot ever be removed from my physical being. You are with me and in me forever more.

'I'm really delighted that you got your wish to go before me, and avoided being left alone, without love or support.

'Being happy for you overrides my need to shed tears.

'Goodbye George, my love. Thanks for my eternal pleasure.'

Epilogue

A beautiful Funeral Mass was held in St Mary's R.C. Church in Greenock, which was well attended, including many friends who were not of the same faith, followed by interment in Knocknairshill Cemetery.

One of the social clubs in which George had spent many happy hours dancing was where the funeral breakfast was held. I wandered around every table and thanked all attendees for showing their respect towards George for the many years during which he enjoyed himself in their company.

Around three weeks after the funeral, something totally unexpected happened, whilst I was sleeping one night.

It seemed as though I had some kind of trauma which kept repeating itself, over and over, until it caused me to wake up.

It wasn't a dream. That was obvious as there were no visual images in my memory. Once I realised what had transpired, I knew that I needed to get up, and write down every repetitive word I had heard, before I forgot any of them.

This trauma was actually all the words, and the tune, of a song which told me how I unconsciously felt about losing George.

The title of this song was "Life will never be the same."

I never thought such a thing was possible. Details listed below.

What am I supposed to do, now that you've gone
What am I supposed to do, now I'm left alone
You no longer come to me, when I call out your name
What am I supposed to do, life will never be the same.

We had a wonderful life, together you and I
And I'd do it all again, in the blink of an eye
But that just cannot be, 'cos fate played its part
Now I'm left alone, with my broken heart.

I hope that you heard me say, 'I love you' and 'Goodbye'
As I sat at your bedside, trying hard not to cry
You could light up every room, with that wonderful smile
Now I only have memories, to last me for a while.

The Lord had other plans for you, but I just don't know why
But I know it would hurt you, that you couldn't say goodbye
They tell me that life goes on, and I know that might be true
But life will never be the same, living without you.

The first time I met you, we were just meant to be
Together forever, till eternity
I'm proud to have held you, in my arms every day
Now life will never be the same, no never, no way.

Now life will never be the same, no never, no way.

This unexpected trauma, for want of a better word, which I had no control over as I was sound asleep, proved to me that we had much more than just a loving relationship between us, we were blessed to also have a spiritual bond between us which cemented us together for forty-six years.

Whilst George was worried about losing me, it wasn't just due to our age difference, he knew about my serious lung problem.

He loved me and cared for me so much, that he would just worry in silence, in order not to put pressure on me.

He was wise enough to know how upset I'd be if I had to keep telling him not to worry, that I'd be OK.

Due to my pulmonary fibrosis, I was unable to sing the song myself, and therefore arranged for it to be produced as a demo disc by a professional singer. I was so happy with the outcome that I realised I wanted to write some songs centred around our life together.

Although I had never thought about song writing before, I found it relatively easy to do, especially as I was inspired by my love for George. I arranged for the same singer to produce each song onto demo discs, for an agreed fee.

The list of songs written by me follows on below.

I Celebrate: Beside Me: I'm Here: My Life was Blessed: In the 175: Love Has the Power: Touch My Heart: First Love: Epitaph: It's a Different World: Our Sapphire Ring: Just Imagine Heaven: Take My Hand: When Love Was Born: The Hand You Used to Hold: Thief in the Night: The Best of its Kind: Your Caring Shadow: Our Breathless Love: Little Boy Blue.

I now have many wonderful memories of my darling, lots of great photos on the walls, and all these great songs to listen to.

There's never a time when George is not on my mind, and, as a result, he brought the happiness of heaven into my life.

Whilst many famous lovers are remembered in history, no amount of love could ever surpass that shared by those known as

GEORGE & HUGH.

www.ingramcontent.com/pod-product-compliance
Lightning Source LLC
Chambersburg PA
CBHW022116090426
42743CB00008B/882